SAN FRANCISCO
VALUES

Common Ground for Getting America Back on Track

GERI SPIELER AND RICK KAPLOWITZ

Palmetto Publishing Group
Charleston, SC

San Francisco Values
Copyright © 2020 by Geri Spieler and Rick Kaplowitz

All rights reserved

First Edition

Printed in the United States

ISBN-13: 978-1-64111-745-6
ISBN-10: 1-64111-745-1

Contents

Introduction

More than 26 million visitors travel to San Francisco each year, 23 million from other parts of this country, and three million from abroad.

They come to explore and enjoy the vibrancy and inviting openness of this legendary California site, to see for themselves why eight million people have chosen to make the Bay Area their home, and to see why so much of what becomes the norm across the country begins in this innovative context.

At the same time, conservative commentators from Bill O'Reilly to the blogger next door have tried to make "San Francisco Values" the three dirtiest words in politics. They use that phrase as a shorthand for plastering an anti-American label on anyone supporting the secular progressive culture commonly associated with the San Francisco Bay Area.

"Hey, look, these are tax-raising, terrorist-loving, same-sex marriage supporting, ultra-liberal Democrats who aren't like you and me," claims Republican media strategist Dan Schnur.

The reality, as this book demonstrates, is that our cherished San Francisco values have much in common with the nation's values; that we are indeed one nation, with our strengths, our limitations, and our aspirations; and that we provide leadership on many issues.

As the *Christian Science Monitor* wrote about San Francisco representative and Speaker of the House Nancy Pelosi:

> Make no mistake: Nancy Pelosi is the most powerful woman in American politics and the most powerful House Speaker since Sam Rayburn a half century ago.

Could the conservatives' fear of this woman's strength and effectiveness be the reason that, in the 2018 elections, Nancy Pelosi was the target in 34% of all GOP broadcast ads aired in House races across the country, ads that painted her as the "poster woman" for everything wrong in America?

A few years earlier, Fox commentator Bill O'Reilly had proclaimed:

> Listen, citizens of San Francisco...if al-Qaida comes in here and blows you up, we're not going to do anything about it. We're going to say, look, every other place in America is off limits to you, except San Francisco. You want to blow up the Coit Tower? Go ahead.

An impressive lineup that includes former House Speakers Newt Gingrich and Dennis Hastert has sought to convince the country that San Francisco is an un-American and evil place.

These comments have as much validity as the suggestions that all those who voted for Donald Trump are racists.

That is, we are bombarded with a whole lot of crap.

However, these ad hominem attacks — that is, attacks directed against individuals rather than the positions they are maintaining — do serve to illustrate how far off track our country has gone. They can help us understand the sources and bases of the toxic and hate-inducing views that have replaced dialog about the real issues facing us.

Let's review America's complex and sometimes conflicting values, and trace how San Francisco values, like other American values, are family-friendly, equality-based, and patriotic. Examine with us the range of sometimes surprising truths that span the nation's political spectrum. Remember that we have been a society that has often managed to find middle ground for addressing problems facing us, and that we can function that way again as we move forward. Consider how the "Action Steps" delineated at the end of each chapter can help each of us realistically evaluate our fundamental issues before going to the polls.

CHAPTER 1

America's Real Values

The U.S. refugee and asylee population paid $63 billion more in taxes than they received in benefits to all levels of government from 2005 to 2014.

— *U.S Department of Health and Human Services*

The overriding impact of immigrants is to strengthen and enrich American culture, increase the total output of the economy, and raise the standard of living of American citizens.

— *David Bier and Alex Nowrasteh, Cato Institute*

Embracing cultural distance, cultural-distance nationalism, means, in effect, taking the position that our country will be better off with more whites and fewer non-whites.

— *Amy Wax, University of Penn Law School Professor; Graduate of Yale, Harvard Medical School, and Columbia Law School*

Values are a society's collective ideas of right and wrong, good and bad, desirable and undesirable behaviors.

Values can be *descriptive*, simply telling what is, or *aspirational*, reflecting who we want to be.

The documents that our Founding Fathers drafted and adopted in forming our government included many compromises, mostly bridging conservative and liberal positions and beliefs.

At this point, 230 years later, we see more of a partisan distribution, where common ground has become much harder to find.

Stereotypes have the effect of widening the divide. Claiming that sanctuary cities love terrorists, or that all Republicans love assault rifles, is clearly inaccurate. Further, they make dialog, and the search for common ground, much more difficult to reach.

The three quotations above show that unanticipated perspectives can be found across that divide. The conservative Cato Institute affirmed the valuable contributions of immigrants, while a white nationalist position is espoused by an Ivy League university faculty member.

Briefly exploring three pairs of conflicting American values can illustrate and help us examine some of the complexities of who we have been, who we are now, and who we want to be. These are:

- Personal achievement and Humanitarianism
- Equality and Race
- Religious faith and Individual freedom

Personal Achievement and Humanitarianism

During his eight years in office, beginning in January 2011, Republican Representative Sean Duffy, of Wisconsin's large, rural 7th Congressional District, voted repeatedly to destroy Obamacare. He also voted for a 2017 bill that would have made insurance coverage less available and/or more expensive for those with pre-existing conditions and voted against the Protecting Americans with Preexisting Conditions Act of 2019.

In September 2019, Duffy announced that he was going to retire from Congress, and that part of his planning was to make sure that his family had coverage for his about-to-be-born daughter's anticipated open-heart surgery — that is, they will have and use medical insurance coverage, insurance that covers preexisting conditions, which is available to him and his family because of Obamacare.

Duffy grew happy to lean on the safety net offered by a [liberally sponsored] government program in order to get the help that he, or any other family, might need when encountering conditions beyond their personal control. That's a more constructive way to look at what could otherwise simply be dismissed as hypocrisy.

Reaching for the American Dream

The American Dream has been described as the opportunity for personal achievement that enables people to move above the economic level they were born into. Success that is based on one's efforts, rather than on rank or riches of family, is strongly valued by conservatives. And it's respected by liberals.

A larger structure often needs to be in place for such personal successes to be possible, as, for example, the truck driver who needs and uses the roads built by the government in order to build and sustain a successful trucking company.

A child may be born with a disease that require resources beyond those available to most families. Having the resources of a collective governmental program that cares for those who are not able to care for themselves is important to liberals. And it's drawn upon by conservatives.

Some suggest that such aid can be abused by those not willing to do their own hard work. Some others will point out that, while some at the lower end of the spectrum may cheat by hiding a bit of income in order to qualify for assistance, the major fraud cases are those in which members of the medical community lie via phantom and fraudulent billing in order to collect millions of dollars for non-provided medical services.

An apocryphal tale has two parts that highlight some of the fallacies of each position if taken to an extreme:

> A man is drowning 50 feet from the end of a dock.

> A conservative rescuer on the dock sees the man and calls out: "I have 25 feet of rope here. You need to swim the first 25 feet on your own, and then I'll throw you the rope for the rest of the way."

[Liberals may be heard laughing here.]

A liberal rescuer on the dock sees the same drowning man and generously throws 75 feet of rope out to him. Then the rescuer drops his end of the rope and goes off to see who else he can help.

[Conservatives may be heard laughing here.]

Perhaps we can all find a more balanced perspective in Georgia's state motto: "Wisdom, justice, and moderation."

A Healthy Nation

The San Francisco Bay Area values entrepreneurs, people like Steve Jobs, who built their fortunes based on their own wisdom and hard work. (These values are reflected in depth in chapter 3, which discusses how the Bay Area business environment effectively supports innovation and growth.)

San Francisco also values the social safety net that is there to help those in our society who are not able to make it on their own. In the medical arena, for example, San Francisco is committed to health care access for all residents. "Healthy San Francisco" became the first municipal American government program designed to provide health insurance for all of its residents. Started in 2007, it operates for those San Francisco residents age 18 or older with income up to 500% of the federal poverty level who are uninsured and ineligible for Medi-Cal or Medicare.

Similarly, at the state level, Massachusetts passed legislation in 2006 providing medical insurance to almost all of its state's residents. The program, signed by Republican Governor Mitt Romney, served in large part as a model for the 2010 national Affordable Care Act (ACA), signed by Democratic President Barack Obama.

The ACA, commonly referred to as "Obamacare," was guided to passage by San Francisco representative and Speaker of the House Nancy Pelosi. It was passed to make coverage for medical costs available to those who did not have such coverage through their employment or similar insurance programs. In addition to enabling medical insurance coverage for some 20 million previously uninsured Americans, it provided coverage for pre-existing conditions, improved coverage of prescription costs for those on Medicare, and allowed children to remain on their parents' medical insurance to age 26.

As Republicans continue to try to dismantle Obamacare, it might help them reconsider that position to know that 68% of the country, most likely including Sean Duffy, wants protection against losing insurance because of pre-existing conditions.

And the number of people who lost their medical insurance as a result of coronavirus layoffs may convince some people to consider more favorably a medical care system that covers all of us, rather than one that is heavily dependent on medical insurance coverage that comes as an employment benefit.

Obamacare was designed as part of the safety net to make insurance for medical care available to all citizens. The implementation of the ACA became highly politicized, with "red" Republican-leaning states choosing to oppose the act and not implement the expanded Medicare option, and "blue" Democratic-leaning states moving forward to make it available to their citizens.

Missouri has been a political swing state throughout the 20th and into the 21st century. Its state motto is "Let the welfare of the people be the supreme law." While 57% of eligible and previously uninsured residents in Missouri did enroll for medical insurance under the ACA, the Missouri legislature, which has been heavily Republican since 2001, has not opted to take advantage of the ACA opportunity to expand Medicaid. Therefore, about 23% of potentially eligible uninsured residents fall into a so-called "coverage gap." This means that they make too much to qualify for Medicaid, but too little to qualify for income-based subsides to buy coverage on the ACA's Healthcare.gov, the federal exchange for individual plans.

Does this approach help provide for "the welfare of the people" of Missouri?

The ACA, including the enhanced Medicaid option, has proven its value. In September 2019, *JAMA: The Journal of the American Medical Association* reported:

> An increasing number of studies have provided rigorous evidence that Medicaid expansion, which has increased the number of Medicaid recipients by more than

10 million since 2013, has been associated with improved health of low-income US residents in various ways, including self-reported health, acute and chronic disease outcomes, and mortality reductions.

It would appear that those state governments that chose to adopt the ACA's opportunity to expand Medicaid did, indeed, provide more adequately for the welfare of their citizens than Missouri and other non-participating states.

Race and Equality

The Declaration of Independence of the United States was ratified on July 4, 1776. It begins with this phrase: "We hold these truths to be self-evident, that all men are created equal."

Many of the men who signed that statement were themselves slave owners. This contradiction between actuality and aspirations may be ascribed to hypocrisy, to a societally ingrained belief that dark-skinned Africans were less human, or to a simple reflection of the reality of that era. In any event, it clearly delineates that not all were seen or treated as equals...not in 1776, and still not in the United States today.

The Articles of Confederation, the first governing document for the confederated states, was created on November 15, 1777, and ratified on March 1, 1781. Article IV stated that "the free inhabitants of each of these states, paupers, vagabonds and fugitives from justice excepted...shall be entitled to all privileges and immunities of free citizens in the several states."

On September 17, 1787, the Constitution of the United States was approved to replace the Articles of Confederation, and it was ratified by the necessary nine of thirteen states by June 21, 1788. Article I, section II, read that when we counted the people in each state, the count was to "be determined by adding to the whole Number of free Persons, including those bound to Service for a Term of Years, and excluding Indians not taxed, three-fifths of all other Persons." A dark-skinned person was thereby counted as three-fifths of a white person.

Voting rights evolved over the years. At first, each state was able to determine its own voters. Those voters were generally white male landowners or white men with equivalent personal property. Free Negroes were initially allowed to vote in several northern states, but those rights were lost in the first part of the 19th century.

Property rights requirements for men were gradually eliminated, state by state, a process that was completed in 1856. In 1868, following the Civil War, the Fourteenth Amendment granted citizenship to "all persons born or naturalized in the United States," but it would take the Fifteenth Amendment in 1870 to establish: "The right of citizens of the United States to vote shall not be denied or abridged by the United States or by any State on account of race, color, or previous condition of servitude."

Women were allowed to vote in the Wyoming Territory. When Wyoming applied to become a state,

Congress demanded that that right to vote be rescinded. Wyoming's famous answer: "We will remain out of the union one hundred years rather than come in without the women." When the Wyoming, Utah, and Washington territories, which allowed women to vote, became states, their women retained that right.

The Nineteenth Amendment, ratified in 1920, was the culmination of a movement toward national female suffrage that began in 1848. The amendment established "that the right of citizens of the United States to vote shall not be denied or abridged by the United States or by any State on account of sex."

We have a significant history of incorporating inequality in our government, and into our laws. Legislation to prevent Chinese immigration, and to prevent Chinese residents from becoming citizens, was in effect from 1882 until 1943. In the 1920s, using arguments based on specious eugenics which declared the inferiority of Jews, Italians, and other immigrants from Southern and Eastern Europe, new legislation imposed strict quotas on immigration from those regions; many of those laws and regulations lasted until 1965.

The inhumanity of slavery has been extensively documented, along with the continued unequal treatment of African Americans in the century and a half following the Civil War. Jim Crow laws in the South, and federal government laws as well, incorporated those biases.

Homeownership and education have long been seen as ways for Americans to begin to build a solid financial base for their families. However, the Federal Housing Administration (FHA), established in 1934, furthered governmental support of segregation efforts by refusing to insure mortgages in and near African American neighborhoods — a policy known as "redlining." At the same time, the FHA was subsidizing builders who were mass-producing entire subdivisions for whites — with the requirement that none of the homes be sold to African Americans.

The GI Bill, passed after World War II as a way to enable returning troops to catch up in the economy for their time in service, provided education and housing and unemployment benefits — but it was not uniformly applied. For example:

- Black veterans in a vocational training program at a segregated high school in Indianapolis were unable to participate in activities related to plumbing, electricity, and printing because adequate equipment was only available to white students. At the college level, 95% of black veterans were shunted off to black colleges.
- Only two of the more than 3,200 VA-guaranteed home loans in 13 Mississippi cities in 1947 went to black borrowers. In New York and the northern New Jersey suburbs, fewer than 100 of the 67,000 mortgages insured by the GI Bill supported home purchases by non-whites.

And things are still unequal. In 2018, black and Asian applicants in Camden, New Jersey, were respectively 2.6 and 1.8 times more likely than whites to be denied home loans, even after adjustments for income, loan amount, and neighborhood.

Thomas Hofeller, the key 21st century Republican strategist on political mapping, conducted dozens of intensely detailed studies of North Carolina college students broken down by race, and then evaluated his data to determine whether these students were likely voters. Based on his findings, the gerrymandered congressional-district line in Greensboro, North Carolina, cuts A&T State University, the nation's largest historically black college, in half. The district line divided this campus — and the city — so precisely that it all but guaranteed that the area would be represented in Congress by two Republicans for years to come. In October 2019, a North Carolina state court found this districting so egregious that it set aside the district lines drawn, sending the process back to be repaired.

Religious Faith and Individual Freedom

In his 1941 State of the Union Address, President Franklin Roosevelt listed four freedoms that he believed everyone in the world should be able to enjoy. Freedom of worship, long a tenet of American life, was one of those.

James Madison wrote, "The Religion then of every man must be left to the conviction and conscience of every man; and it is the right of every man to exercise it as these may dictate. This right is in its nature an unalienable right."

This concept was incorporated into the governing documents of the United States.

Article VI of the Constitution states: "No religious Test shall ever be required as a Qualification to any Office or public Trust under the United States."

And the First Amendment to the Constitution states: "Congress shall make no law respecting an establishment of religion, or prohibiting the free exercise thereof."

Peter Manseau wrote for the *Smithsonian* that the persecution that Puritans faced in England was a key factor driving them to the New World. He added that this was also true for Quakers, Baptists, Shakers, Jews, and other religious minorities, all of whom saw America as a place they would finally be free to practice their faith.

Kenneth Davis, also writing for *Smithsonian* magazine, reached even more deeply, stating that the "idea that the United States has always been a bastion of religious freedom is reassuring — and utterly at odds with the historical record." His examples include the following:

- The Puritan fathers of the Massachusetts Bay Colony did not countenance tolerance of opposing religious views. Their "city upon a hill" was a theocracy that brooked no dissent, religious or political.
- Catholics ("Papists") were anathema and were banned from the colonies, along with other non-Puritans. And the anti-Catholicism of America's Calvinist past would find new voice in the 19th century as well.
- Four Quakers were hanged in Boston between 1659 and 1661 for persistently returning to the city to stand up for their beliefs.

- In Massachusetts, only Christians were allowed to hold public office, and Catholics were allowed to do so only after renouncing papal authority. In 1777, New York State's constitution banned Catholics from public office (and would do so until 1806). In Maryland, Catholics had full civil rights, but Jews did not. Delaware required an oath affirming belief in the Trinity.
- In 1832, a mob tarred and feathered Joseph Smith, marking the beginning of a long battle between Christian America and Smith's Mormonism.
- America's anti-Semitism was practiced institutionally as well as socially for decades.
- With the great threat of "godless" Communism looming in the 1950s, the country's fear of atheism also reached new heights.

In *Democracy in America*, Alexis de Tocqueville's summary of his nine-month US visit in 1831, he observed:

> They all attributed the peaceful dominion of religion in their country mainly to the separation of church and state. I do not hesitate to affirm that during my stay in America I did not meet a single individual, of the clergy or the laity, who was not of the same opinion on this point.

Religion can be seen from the micro level, in terms of how it impacts individual day-to-day living, all the way to the macro level of its impact on countries and on wars among and across nations and continents. It has been suggested that many wars were fought for religious reasons. Others, such as Rabbi Alan Lurie, suggest that the vast majority of wars were started for territorial conquest, to control borders, to secure trade routes, or to respond to an internal challenge to political authority. In their introduction to the extensively detailed *Encyclopedia of Wars*, authors Charles Phillips and Alan Axelrod make the point that, while the reasons most wars were started were not for religion, for those who fought in them, "for much of the world before the 17th century, these 'reasons' for war were explained and justified, at least for the participants, by religion."

A significant number of recent international conflicts have been framed as being between adherents of Christianity and those of Islam. Major conflicts between Hindus and Muslims have riven Southern Asia, and the wars between the Sunni and Shia sects of Islam in the Middle East have been ongoing since the 7th century. Religious conflicts are strongly juxtaposed on other social issues in 21st century America, impacting such basic areas of focus as elections, governance, and medicine.

From its founding, the United States has been a majority white Christian country. As that demographic fact gradually continues to evolve, the so-called "evangelical" segment of the population has been the focus of much attention as it struggles to define its values and express its concerns.

Many of the issues that were addressed during the formation of our nation were settled by compromise. However, as Dan Barker notes on the Americans United

website (au.com), while many of our Founding Fathers
were Christian believers themselves, their answer to
the question "Is America a Christian nation?" was clearly
"No." Barker writes:

> The U.S. Constitution is a wholly secu-
> lar document. It contains no mention of
> Christianity or Jesus Christ. In fact, the
> Constitution refers to religion only twice
> in the First Amendment, which bars laws
> "respecting an establishment of religion
> or prohibiting the free exercise thereof,"
> and in Article VI, which prohibits "religious
> tests" for public office. Both of these provi-
> sions are evidence that the country was not
> founded as officially Christian.

In a 1790 letter celebrating the fact that Jews had
full freedom to worship in America, George Washington
wrote, "All possess alike liberty of conscience and immunities of citizenship." And Article XI of a 1797 treaty
unanimously approved by Congress also states that the
"government of the United States is not, in any sense,
founded on the Christian religion."

Has America remained true to our founders' vision of
religious and individual freedom?

In 1985, Supreme Court Justice John Paul Stevens,
writing the decision in *Wallace v. Jaffree*, stated:

> When the underlying principle has been
> examined in the crucible of litigation, the

Court has unambiguously concluded that the individual freedom of conscience protected by the First Amendment embraces the right to select any religious faith or none at all.

In his book, *The End of White Christian America*, Dr. Robert P. Jones examines the political and cultural changes among evangelicals, particularly over the past 25 years, calling them a "disaffected group that is anxious to hold onto a white, conservative Christian culture that is passing from the scene."

Drawing upon Jones's work and more, a *Time* magazine article looks at how Trump received evangelical support in defeating primary opponents with much stronger Christian credentials — Huckabee, Santorum, Cruz, and Rubio among them — and in his contest with lifelong Methodist Hillary Clinton. The article then goes on to discuss how white evangelicals' early and steadfast support for Trump has changed them, particularly when it comes to their views on values.

In 2011, and again five years later, Jones's Public Religion Research Institute asked Americans if a political leader who "committed an immoral act in his or her private life could nonetheless behave ethically and fulfill their duties in their public life."

Their findings:

- In 2011, only 30% of white evangelical Protestants agreed with this statement, a response consistent with the so-called "values voter," who placed a priority on a candidate's moral character.

- In 2016, a staggering 72% of white evangelists responded they believe a candidate can build a kind of "moral wall" between his private and public life.

As the researchers noted,

> In a shocking reversal, white evangelicals have gone from being the least likely to the most likely group to agree that a candidate's personal immorality has no bearing on his performance in public office...This about face is stunning, especially against the backdrop of white evangelicals' outrage in response to Bill Clinton's indiscretions in the 1990's...Rather than standing on principle and letting the chips fall where they may, white evangelicals have now fully embraced a consequentialist ethics that works backward from predetermined political ends, refashioning or even discarding principles as needed to achieve a desired outcome.

It would appear that at least some of those Americans who vote on the basis of their religious beliefs are currently in the midst of examining, and possibly reevaluating, the relationship between their religious values and their national values.

In the United States today, there are major movements to impose the values and beliefs of certain Christian sects upon all residents of the country. No issue is more clearly illustrative than that of each individual's control of and responsibility for their own physical and mental health, and that issue is played out in large part on rules relating to abortion, and in other rules governing women's (but not men's) bodies.

Sharia law is the code for living that is set out by Islam for its followers, and it includes penalties for failures to adhere. Sharia is applied to legislation, in at least some form, in some fifty-three different Muslim jurisdictions and countries, and fifteen countries are actually governed by these principles.

There has been conflict between those practices and international human rights norms, particularly with respect to cruel and inhumane punishments.

While there have been no active movements to implement sharia law in the United States, seven states—Alabama, Arizona, Kansas, Louisiana, North Carolina, South Dakota, and Tennessee—have acted to ban sharia law or passed some kind of ballot measure prohibiting state courts from considering religious law.

Yet two of those very same states (and seven more) still have unenforced laws on the books prohibiting abortion. And a number of other states have recently passed restrictive legislation on abortion, seeking to force a review and, ultimately, a reversal of the *Roe v. Wade* decision upholding abortion rights. Supporters of those restrictive laws are heavily drawn from among the evangelicals—a segment of Christians legally seeking to impose their religiously-based values, via governmental rules, on individual sovereignty over one's body.

The San Francisco Bay Area ethos strongly values the rights of individuals to make their own medical decisions.

While some might wish to suggest that these values reflect an antireligious bias, they are held by people of many religions, and by people who choose not to worship any deity.

Consider, for example, the Church of the Sojourners, an Intentional Christian Community located in San Francisco that has long included evangelical Protestants, mainline Protestants, and Catholics. They do not identify with either the "Christian right" or the "Christian left," but try to navigate by the ways Jesus called people to be faithful.

The Sojourners compare American Christianity to the Pharisees, "obsessed with their holy scripture while completely ignoring the loving God it was intended to direct them to," saying:

> When LGBTQ individuals, people of color, immigrants, refugees, 'foreigners,' Muslims, and others faced societal injustices, the white church not only was largely absent from defending them, but it was complicit to their persecution...In the face of such injustices, Jesus became furious and overturned tables. He drove out the moneychangers and condemned the spiritual leaders of his day.

The Sojourners remind people of Matthew's gospel teaching: to "love your neighbor as yourself."

America's Values

In 1831, de Tocqueville identified five core American values.

1. Liberty: Freedom of doing anything one chooses as long as someone else's liberty isn't taken away.
2. Egalitarianism: The belief that all humans have equal rights and equal say.
3. Individualism: The belief that people are free to choose and work toward their own goals independently from other people.
4. Populism: The idea that the common people have the same rights and opportunity as the elite in society.
5. Laissez-faire: The belief that the government should not interfere in economic affairs of the country.

A century and a half later, sociologist Robin M. Williams summarized his findings of traditional American values in his widely referenced work that included fifteen core items. Williams himself pointed out that these values are sometimes contradictory.

Williams' list of values can be gathered into three groups:

- Liberty and justice for all: freedom, democracy, equality, but also racism and group superiority
- Success in our culture: individualism, personal achievement, work, efficiency and practicality, science and technology, and progress

- The American social context: material comfort, humanitarianism, education, religious faith, romantic love

Our country has maintained a fairly steady course over these years, sustaining its growth through national expansion and international wars. Questions about these values today reflect significant challenges that the country faces in this 21st century.

As these examples illustrate, and other chapters amplify, most San Francisco values are a mix of descriptive and aspirational, as they are in most parts of the country. America's national values speak to individual freedom and to religious freedom. We value and seek to reward the self-motivated individual achievers, and to care for those not as able to care for themselves.

San Francisco values do express aspirations for racial equality, for an inclusion of all ethnic and social groups, and for individual freedoms including those relating to gender identity and to medical choice. There is the hope that, as in so many other things, those who don't yet hold these tenets for our country will gradually see the wisdom of these San Francisco values.

Take Action

1. **Your values.** Think about your own values and how you want to see them reflected in our laws. Do the people in or running for office say they want the same things? If so, do they act in ways that match their words? Do they say they want health coverage without limits on pre-existing

conditions, or that they want a comprehensive immigration policy, but vote otherwise? Support candidates who truly support your values.

2. **One-issue voting.** A number of us tend to pick one issue and focus on that. If you have one such issue that is very important to you, does that make all other issues insignificant? Do you sometimes vote for candidates who represent that one value, even when their other positions do not serve your best interests, or serve party over country? Consider candidates who best represent your overall interests.

3. **Religion.** The history of our nation is deeply imbued in a separation of Church and State, derived in large part by our founders who wanted to avoid the mistakes of many European and Asian governments of the time. You don't want others to tell you what religion you may or may not practice. Similarly, don't try to impose your religion on others. Share your religious values and beliefs with your children, and allow others to do the same for theirs. Seek candidates who espouse the rule of secular law, not religious law.

4. **Personal behavior.** Can there really be a wall between an elected official's personal and public life? At what point does the personal behavior and morality of an elected official become a matter of public concern? Were you, as a parent, comfortable explaining President Bill Clinton's extra-marital behavior to your kids? Are you, as a parent,

comfortable in explaining President Donald Trump's bullying behaviors and frequent lies to your children? We aren't perfect, and we can't expect those we elect to be perfect. On the other hand, do consider whether you think our leaders should be expected to be reasonable role models for us, and evaluate whether those on the ballot do indeed behave with the decency and perhaps even wisdom we would want our children to learn.

CHAPTER 2

The Evolution of Values, San Francisco Style

One day if I do go to heaven,
I'll look around and say,
'It ain't bad, but it ain't San Francisco.'
— *Herb Caen*

If you're alive, you can't be bored in San Francisco.
If you're not alive, San Francisco will bring you to life.
— *William Saroyan*

So, how did San Francisco become San Francisco? And, what exactly are San Francisco's values?

San Francisco grew rapidly during the gold rush, with immigrants from Europe, Japan, China, and South America, as well as the US East Coast, creating a city virtually overnight. They depended on each other to build a society in which they could live and work. It was the proverbial melting pot, where their common needs outweighed any differences.

This chapter identifies ten key values that evolved in the San Francisco Bay Area and traces how San Francisco became a leader in progressive ideals and came to lead the country and the world technically and socially. Following chapters examine some of these values in greater depth, in the area and across the nation.

San Francisco Values

- **Personal freedom in love and marriage is bedrock.** San Franciscans don't impose political or religious bounds on each person's right to express their own humanity, their own sexual identity, and their freedom to love others as they choose, and to build families in their myriad possible structures.
- **We support our military.** The San Francisco Bay Area has always supported our uniformed troops, both during and after their service. Of equal import, San Franciscans actively examine and, as appropriate, question the political rationales that may be put forward for military action. Democracy, individualism, and patriotism are part of this values cluster.
- **Personal sovereignty — that is, our bodies belong to us.** Each individual has personal sovereignty, which includes that person's right to choose their medical providers and to make informed decisions about medical, social, and related sexual options and choices.
- **Cannabis is a valid personal medical and recreational choice.** California recognizes individual

choice with respect to marijuana and supports additional valid scientific study on its impact on the body. This includes seeking to correct the artificial, erroneous, and invalid federal categorization of marijuana as a Schedule 1 drug.

- **Technological innovation and industrial creativity are respected and supported.** The Bay Area social and corporate environment provides a supportive context within which world leadership in electronic and biochemical technology has evolved.
- **We embrace and value the richness of our human differences.** We are a diverse nation of immigrants, the broad amalgam of people who have built our country, and who continue to contribute to our strength in so many ways. We celebrate the contributions of each of the many individuals and cultures that meet and merge here.
- **Integrity.** Hypocrisy undercuts both personal and public trust. The San Francisco Bay Area appreciates people who respectfully live their lives with integrity, in accordance with the values they express, so long as those values don't diminish or subvert the liberty and equality of others. Mixed feelings, both sadness and a sense of "aha, we knew something was wrong," are evoked when people loudly oppose certain behaviors in others and are subsequently found to be practicing those same behaviors they have excoriated.
- **We value and support the creative arts.** The arts flourish in the Bay Area's environment, which

is supportive of open expression. The literary community is vibrant, and governmental and private support for visual and orchestral expressions abound.

- **We are willing to work to find good ways to fix what is broken.** Problems exist in this city, as in others across the country. Homelessness and drugs do diminish the quality of life for all. We are optimistically willing to work — and work and work — to develop programs and policies to address these seemingly intractable problems. We seek to recognize and draw upon scientific knowledge to help us identify and develop solutions for our problems.

- **As Americans, as well as San Franciscans, we continue to aspire to freedom, equality, and opportunity for all.** We continue to strive to move, together, toward becoming the best of what we, as human beings and as a nation, can be.

San Franciscans reflects such truly American values as family, individuality, loyalty, patriotism, scientific creativity, diversity, and the use of public policy for the public good. It is when these values are explored, understood, and embraced, rather than mindlessly caricatured, that San Francisco's vibrant affirmation of our national ethic and posture can be fully appreciated. When these perspectives are affirmed, rather than feared and shunned, they can help individuals reconnect and bring some measure of peace to the war of words that divide us.

Let us begin by tracing the evolution of the modern San Francisco Bay Area.

The Growth of San Francisco

Many visitors reach San Francisco by driving up the magnificent coastal highways from the south that include Highways 101 and 1. These roads essentially trace the route followed by Father Junipero Serra, the five-foot-two-inch-tall Catholic priest who, between 1769 and 1782, founded nine Catholic missions along the Nueva California coast.

Mission San Francisco de Assis, eventually renamed Mission Dolores, was founded by Father Serra at the mouth of the Golden Gate, in 1776, contemporaneously with the American Declaration of Independence back east.

The Native American Muwekma Ohlone tribe had been resident across the Bay Area at least as far back as 1100 AD, living in the counties now known as San Francisco, San Mateo, Santa Clara, Alameda, and Contra Costa, as well as in portions of Napa, Santa Cruz, Solano, and San Joaquin. Fairly large populations of native peoples have been traced back in the Santa Clara Valley areas over a span of ten thousand years.

For 70 years, Nueva California continued to be part of the territory owned by Spain, and then part of the Republic of Mexico after that nation declared its independence from Spain in 1810.

The US Congress voted to annex Texas, which was also part of Mexico, in 1845, and the Mexican-American War erupted in response to that preemptive legislation.

As one aspect of that war, Commodore John Sloat claimed Nueva California for the United States in July 1846, and Captain John Montgomery specifically claimed the three existing Golden Gate area settlements of Yerba Buena, the Presidio, and Mission Dolores.

An 1846 census of the three Bay Area communities collectively identified 290 residents of Mexican and European descent. Including outposts, but not counting the Ohlone, there were fewer than four hundred people in the area.

On January 24, 1848, John Marshall discovered gold at Captain John A. Sutter's sawmill on the American Fork River. As word got out that "there was gold in them thar hills," San Francisco, the nearest port and cross-country terminus to the gold fields, became a boom town almost overnight. This growth was further spurred by President James Polk's December 1848 message to Congress recognizing the California gold rush.

In 1849, gold hunters poured into San Francisco from all over the world; by the end of that year, the population had reached 23,000 people. San Francisco continued to grow rapidly through the balance of the 19th century, to 150,000 people in 1870, and almost 350,000 people in 1900.

Coming to San Francisco in 1849 was not for the weakhearted or simpleminded. Those who made it were the hardiest, luckiest, and most determined to survive the journey.

The overland route, by covered wagon, took six months, following a winding 2,000 to 3,000-mile trail through prairies and deserts, and across the steep Rocky

Mountains. Many died along the way from starvation, infection, flooded river crossings, contaminated water holes, and attacks by Native Americans or from other wagon trains out to steal provisions.

The alternative route was a journey by sea, down and around Cape Horn, the storied graveyard of many sailing vessels. The trip was 15,000 miles, and it took as long as eight months to go from Boston to San Francisco. A trip across Panama was also attempted by some; those who made it through the jungles to the Pacific, however, did not readily find ships to take them to San Francisco. The Cape Horn route was probably the least treacherous of all the routes to the gold fields.

Despite the difficulties of the journey, people flooded in, by land and sea, by the thousands. Living conditions were suboptimal. The men who came out West to find gold didn't take the time to build anything more than basic living spaces. Few cared about anything except getting to the foothills of the Sierra Mountains and finding gold; those not going out to pan for gold were focused on developing supply sources and services for the miners.

Only the great gambling houses, hotels, restaurants, and a few public buildings had any pretension to size and comfort. The streets were uneven, often knee-deep in mud, and dark at night, as there were no streetlights yet.

The rapid pace of growth had a major impact on the evolution of the city. Even more critical than the speed of growth was the unbalanced nature of the in-migrants. The hardy adventurers who came to San Francisco were, at first, almost all men. Men without families, without the leavening influence of mothers and wives and sisters and daughters. Parental authority figures to tame the wild behavior of the gold miners were not part of the landscape.

Absent families, there was no one to tell the men how to behave, or how to use the correct fork, or how to require other men to treat women who could, in other settings, be their sisters. Displays of poor table manners, mismatched shirts and pants, and a lack of a civil tongue were common on the streets and in the saloons.

When women did begin to arrive, many of them, in turn, were also adventurous — and, for many, their adventures were to provide female company and services to the men. Prostitution was flourishing in every major American city in the second half of the 19th century; with the untamed and unbalanced nature of the growth of the gold (and then silver) adventurers in Northern California, and the easy virtue of that environment, brothels became a special and major factor in the evolution of the San Francisco landscape and soul.

Brothels

The mythological image of the gold rush women in San Francisco depicts bawdy, lavishly dressed prostitutes cavorting all night with hard-drinking miners and gamblers, men who were throwing bags of gold dust on the tables in exchange for the women's attentions and services.

The reality was, of course, more complex. Even so, the economic opportunity of a gold rush prostitute was way beyond that of the average working American female.

Multi-tasking was common for the working women of the gold rush. A woman who wore her one fancy dress while "entertaining" spent the rest of her time in her Levi's jeans, cutting wood, cleaning house, and cooking meals both for the men and for her working sisters.

A wide range of opportunities characterized the business of prostitution in a wide-open setting where there were neither Family Research Councils, nor local unions, nor an established social context.

Some women were disempowered, remaining in the lower echelons as they worked in the hastily constructed cribs of the back alleys of the Barbary Coast area; others gained an unprecedented ascension to power in San Francisco.

Chinese prostitutes were generally indentured servants. Some white women had been kidnapped and enslaved, and many Latina prostitutes were economically and socially oppressed. At the same time, a surge of higher-class European and white American prostitutes recognized and capitalized on the opportunity for upward mobility in the sexually tolerant city.

Some prostitutes became mistresses of the wealthier miners, developing romantic relationships and gaining an increasing degree of respectability.

Caleb T. Fay, a Massachusetts merchant who took a six-month ship voyage around Cape Horn to reach the goldfields in 1849, became an insurance industry leader and local political activist in San Francisco between 1850 and his passing in 1885. Fay noted, "The only aristocracy

we had here at the time was the gamblers and prostitutes." According to Fay:

> Some prostitutes were part of the upper
> echelons of San Francisco society. Not
> only were they the most elegantly dressed
> women in San Francisco...both on the
> street and in the gambling saloons where
> they worked, but they actually set the style
> for the women in the city. Furthermore,
> their social circles involved the most promi-
> nent men in town.

One famous mistress, known only by her first name,
Juanita, gained her notoriety by becoming the first woman to be hanged in California, after she stabbed a man
who was about to attack her lover.

American historian Hubert Howe Bancroft, whose
60,000 volumes became the core of the University of
California at Berkeley's Bancroft library, observed that
"deference was paid by all classes to the female form,
even though its dress covered corruption; nor was it very
damaging to any man's reputation...to be seen in conversation with a public woman."

Further, a culture of prostitutes as entrepreneurs
emerged, with some of the more successful San
Francisco madams and hookers leading the way for
women into other business enterprises, as they became
investors in the rapidly growing city.

San Francisco was tolerant of not only the members
of the prostitution and gambling industries, but also of

those living other alternative lifestyles as well, including homosexuals.

With so few women available as the city grew, the population adopted a "see-no-evil" attitude toward homosexuality.

As there were not enough women to complete the circle at the local dances, some men danced as the female partners. A technique of using colored handkerchiefs in order to separate male and female roles for square dances was created in the saloons of the gold rush era. This use of colored handkerchiefs was adapted beyond temporary roles to signal particular sexual inclinations, spreading to Europe and becoming common in England during the Victorian era, before returning to America's gay communities in the latter half of the 20th century.

Whether they started as prospectors, prostitutes, or suppliers of other services, as gays or straights, most folks traveled out to the wilds of California with one thing in mind: to spend as short a time as possible getting rich and then return home wealthy. While few intended to make California their home, many people changed their minds once there. The weather, the less prohibitive ambiance of San Francisco, and the extraordinary economic growth opportunities induced many to settle in.

The city's explosive growth substantively cramped local government's ability to develop and manage the civic infrastructure normally expected in a city. Construction was shoddy, protective city services such as police and fire were not yet in place, and planning commissions and building codes did not exist.

One result was that San Francisco was heavily damaged by fire six times between 1848 and 1851. Nevertheless, California statehood was achieved in 1850; the Union Pacific and Southern Pacific rail lines were built in the 1860s, providing transcontinental railroad service, and the city continued to grow rapidly during the second half of the 19th century.

At the end of that century, during the 1898 Spanish-American War fought in both the Caribbean and the Pacific, San Francisco's role as a port contributed yet again to the growth of the city and to its particular populations. The city was the homeport to thousands of men heading to the Philippines. These young soldiers found that there were opportunities to earn extra money by escorting admiring older men strolling the South of Market area...and that they could earn even more if they proved serviceable. A number of senior officers were also known to appreciate these accommodating escorts.

Emperor Norton

Always a welcoming city, San Francisco hosted the emergence of many colorful characters over the years. One whose history illustrates San Francisco's tolerance and embrace of the different, the quirky, and the eccentric was English-born Joshua Abraham Norton.

Norton journeyed to San Francisco via South Africa in the mid-1850s. He arrived with some wealth but lost it in a financial deal gone sour. Shortly thereafter, in 1859, he proclaimed himself Imperial Majesty Emperor Norton I, Emperor of these United States.

As described on a Voice of America broadcast:

> Emperor Norton usually did not have any money. But he did not need any. If Emperor Norton went to a restaurant, he was served a meal — free. If he needed something little from a store, that was also freely given. Sometimes he paid with his own kind of money...paper money with his picture on it.

Some stores began placing a small sign in their windows, reading: "By Appointment to His Majesty, Emperor Norton the First." Stores with these signs noted that their business increased.

Friends and neighbors glorified Norton's regal presence, in his self-designed blue and gold uniform. His proclamations were announced in the local press, including his "order" that the US Congress be dissolved by force. His "decrees," while sometimes compelling in content, had no power in fact. Yet his presence was felt as a strong part of the city's ethos.

At one point, a group organized an anti-Chinese committee, which set out to foment violence in the city's Chinese neighborhoods. One night, members of the committee left a meeting and walked toward the area of the city where most of the Chinese lived. As they got close to the area, one man stood in the street blocking their way. He said nothing. He did not move. The mob of troublemakers stopped. They looked at Emperor Norton, standing in his old blue uniform with its gold-colored buttons. They said nothing. They did nothing. Slowly, the mob turned and walked away.

Businesses closed in San Francisco on the day of Emperor Norton's funeral in 1880, and more than 10,000 people attended his burial ceremony.

By 1900, the population of San Francisco had grown to 342,782, making the city the most populous in California and the ninth most populous city nationwide.

The other five counties in the immediate San Francisco Bay area continued, during the last half of the 19th century, to provide agricultural products to San Francisco and beyond.

Monterey hosted California's Constitutional Convention. San Jose, at the southern tip of San Francisco Bay, was designated as the first capital of the state of California, but the town did not have the amenities to house delegates, and the capital was quickly moved to Vallejo, and then Benicia, and then, in 1854, to Sacramento.

Paper was produced in Marin (just north of San Francisco), oil wells produced in Santa Clara County for a fifteen-year period, and the city of Oakland, just across the bay, grew to 67,000 by 1900.

Higher Education

Developments in one other segment during that period — higher education — would have a profound impact on the nature of the San Francisco Bay Area in the years to follow. In addition to several smaller colleges, three institutions that would earn international recognition were founded: the University of California at Berkeley, the University of California at San Francisco, and Stanford University.

UC Berkeley, founded in 1868, would grow slowly for its first 30 years, until several major Hearst and Strauss gifts supported a major building boom in the late 1890s, expanding the campus significantly. Women were admitted on an equal basis starting in 1871; in 1874, Rosa Scribner was the first woman to graduate. By 1897, Berkeley was offering financial aid to students with need.

Instruction in dentistry was joined with instruction in medicine and pharmacy in 1881, forming the nucleus of the medical faculties at the University of California San Francisco. At the turn of the century, full-time scientific faculty positions in anatomy, pathology, and physiology were created to round out the health-sciences focus of the campus.

In 1884, fifteen-year old Leland Stanford Junior, the only son of railroad magnate and former California governor Leland Stanford and his wife, Jane, died of typhoid fever. His parents visited several major campuses back east for advice and then launched a university in Palo Alto, named in honor of their son.

From the outset, Stanford made some untraditional choices: the university would be coeducational, at a time when most were all-male; non-denominational, when most were associated with a religious organization; and avowedly practical, committed to producing "cultured and useful citizens," when most were concerned only with the former.

The San Francisco Bay Area entered the 20th-century poised to begin making significant contributions to the future of the nation and the world. The city's explosive growth incorporated adventurous, self-sufficient, and independent-minded people, who made their own rules, effectively building a society in a deeply held context of individual rights and choices.

San Francisco burned down six times between 1848 and 1851, well before the Great Earthquake and Fire of 1906. Each time there was a fire, the entire community of Chinese, Mexicans, Chileans, Inca, French, and English, an amalgam that ranged from prostitutes to family members who settled in after the initial gold rush, put aside their differences, came together, and rebuilt the city, over and over and over again. Working with mutual interests in survival, these diverse communities developed a camaraderie and an appreciation for the others that provided a basis for the city's legendary embrace of diversity.

Take Action

1. **Personal sovereignty.** Presuming that you want the right to make your own choices about your own life, and that others should therefore have that same right, look for candidates whose behavior and votes reflect a "live and let live" perspective.
2. **Integrity over hypocrisy.** Examine candidates to see if their behaviors, their stated positions, and their votes match. Value a candidate's honesty, reliability, and integrity above specific policies.

3. **Problem-solving.** We haven't solved all of our problems. Look for candidates who seek to adapt old ways and/or develop new approaches to bring us together in order to solve the problems facing us as a society.
4. **Equality.** Seek candidates who focus on and embrace our common humanity, and on our need for equal opportunities for all, rather than on preferences and differences, made worse with insults, threats, bullying, and discriminatory laws.

CHAPTER 3

Why San Francisco Leads the Nation in Innovation

We invented the martini, the fortune cookie, denim jeans, It's-Its, Irish coffee, the jukebox and Rice-A-Roni. But more important, we're a city that encourages thinking outside the box for solutions. Take the story about the Murphy bed for example. The story goes that William L. Murphy was courting a woman in 1932 who thought it was improper to visit a man's bedroom — but he lived in a one-room studio. So, Murphy invented a bed that could be hidden in the wall frame.

— *Kevin Fisher-Paulson, author and columnist, San Francisco Chronicle*

The United States, which has long taken pride in its "can-do" attitude, continues to be the global leader in science and technology.

The National Science Foundation's *Science and Engineering Indicators* for 2018 indicate that the United States invests the most in research and development, attracts the most venture capital, awards the most advanced degrees, and provides the most business, financial, and information services in the world. The US investment of $496 billion represents 26% of the global total; China has now become second internationally, at 21% ($408 billion).

Much of this activity takes place in the San Francisco Bay Area, which values innovation, accompanied by the willingness to take risks in developing new products and processes. Examples track back to the gold rush era, as exemplified by Levi Strauss, and continue today as reflected in the "gig economy's" Airbnb, developed in San Francisco by Brian Chesky, Joe Gebbia, and Nathan Blechzrczyk.

Strauss was born in Bavaria. He migrated to New York in 1847 to join his family in their dry goods business. He moved west to San Francisco in 1854, where he manufactured and sold tents, along with clothing, bedding, combs, and purses. He found that his customers complained that their pants pockets would rip when subjected to the stress of the various mining tools they would carry in their pockets. Strauss and his customer Jacob Davis explored securing the pockets with rivets, and it was a big success with the mining community. The two men patented the new style of work pants in 1873, and Levi's blue jeans are now worn around the world.

This pioneering spirit, which includes a willingness to fail as an important part of risk-taking and a readiness to learn from those failures, and to try again, has provided a base upon which the Bay Area has become a world leader in both entrepreneurial electronic and biochemical technology, just as it is in social dynamics. A third major industry sector that factors into the dynamism of the area is the preponderant presence of venture capitalists.

We'll examine each of these three sectors and look at the values that nurture innovation more in this region than any other.

Computer Tech

In the 1960s, America's electronic technology was emerging in two key locations: along the Route 128 belt in Massachusetts that curves in an arc with a 15-mile radius around Boston, and on the peninsula south of San Francisco.

Both areas drew upon strong university resources. Cambridge, with Massachusetts Institute of Technology and Harvard University scientists and engineers, fueled the Route 128 developments; Stanford University and its related Palo Alto research community provided the primary core in California. Starting about even in the mid-1960s, California's Silicon Valley, encompassing the area from San Jose to San Francisco, moved significantly beyond the Route 128 center to become the pre-eminent national and international leader in computer tech.

A casual conversation with a very high-level Wang Labs executive in Lowell, Massachusetts, in the latter half of the 1970s, contained a significant foretelling of the shift that was to take place. That Wang policy maker shared what would prove to be the company's mistaken, short-sighted, and fatal perspective: "Small computers are a nice toy, but they can't possibly replace the word processing technology that we have developed for the printing and publishing world."

Several authors have examined and analyzed, in depth, the evolution of the pre-eminence of Silicon Valley.

In her 1994 *Inc.* article "Silicon Valley Versus Route 128," AnnaLee Saxenian, dean of the School of Information at the University of California, Berkeley, details the business crises that simultaneously hit each area when Silicon Valley chip makers were overtaken by the Japanese semiconductor industry and Route 128 minicomputer companies were overtaken by the shift to workstations and personal computers.

Supported by in-depth studies of several specific companies in each setting, Saxenian concludes that Silicon Valley's successful emergence and new growth was built on a culture that values and promotes collective learning and flexible adjustment, and companies that make specialty products within a broad range of related technologies. She also cites the region's social networks and open labor markets, which encourage entrepreneurship and experimentation.

In contrast, the Route 128 region's industrial system contains vertically integrated independent companies that keep largely to themselves. Secrecy and corporate loyalty govern relations between the more traditionally organized companies and their customers, suppliers, and competitors, reinforcing a regional culture that encourages stability and self-reliance, with centralized authority and information that tends to flow vertically only.

Demographics expert Paul Mackun traced industrial evolution in these two areas 25 years later, in his netvalley.com article "Silicon Valley and Route 128: Two Faces of the American Technopolis." In comparing the histories, attitudes, and strategies most conducive to long-term success in the two settings, Mackun observed a direct contrast between the Silicon Valley's "reliance on risk-taking and partnerships" and eastern Massachusetts's "emphasis upon convention, decorum, and self-reliance."

Elizabeth Charnock of Bloomberg focuses on Silicon Valley's unique approach to failure as what makes the region very successful, observing "the mantra adopted by Silicon Valley is 'fail fast' while the rest of the world follows the mantra of 'don't fail.'"

During the "dot-com boom" years between 1995 and 2000, it was not uncommon for Silicon Valley investors to hear venture capital proposals for funding include a statement such as, "Two principals in the new company have each had two previous failures in new ventures, and they've really learned from that."

Ben and Mena Trott had lost their jobs in start-up tech companies in 2003, when they were 24 years old. Without money, but with their faith in their own hands, Mena, who was a graphic artist, journaled her feelings, and she began to toy around with design concepts for her journalizing. Ben, who happened to be a programmer, helped her in the areas where she needed technical advice.

Friends started asking to use Mena's "program," which led to the birth of Six Apart. The company developed several applications that were seminal in the development of the "blog" phenomena. Perhaps lesser known among Silicon Valley innovation stories numbering in the thousands, Mena reflects the "pick yourself up, dust yourself off, and start all over again" San Francisco values of taking risks and of moving beyond failures.

Among the ten-thousand-plus companies in the San Francisco Bay Area that serve the nation and the world, the well-known tech innovators include the following: 23andMe, Adobe Inc., Airbnb, Ancestry, Apple, Ask.com, Autodesk, Barracuda Networks, Cisco, Craigslist, DocuSign, Dropbox, eBay, Evernote, Facebook, Fitbit, Gap, Google, GoPro, Hewlett-Packard, Instacart, Intuit, Jawbone, LinkedIn, Lyft, Marvell Studios, McAfee, Mozilla, Nest Labs, Netflix, Oracle, Palantir Technologies, Quora, Sage, Salesforce, SanDisk, Seagate Technology, Sephora, Silicon Graphics, Slack Technologies, SurveyMonkey, Symantec, Tesla, Twitter, Uber, VMware, Wikimedia, Yahoo!, Yelp, Zillow, and Zynga.

Electronic technology in the region continues to explore at the cutting edge. Crunchbase identifies 626 artificial intelligence companies now functioning in the Silicon Valley area.

Of all the well-known tech innovators, no one is better known or more influential than San Francisco native Steve Jobs. His brilliance and creativity have touched people globally. No matter what language you speak, everyone knows the name Steve Jobs.

Jobs was born in 1955 to Abdulfattah Jandali and Joanne Schieble. Jandali was a Syrian political refugee who came to the United States. He was studying for his PhD in economics at the University of Wisconsin, where he met Schieble. He was a Muslim, she a Catholic. When she became pregnant, she wanted to marry Jandali, but her father did not allow that, so she went to San Francisco, where Steve was born, and where he was adopted by Paul and Clara Jobs.

He grew up in Mountain View, where he learned mechanics and electronics from his dad. He attended Reed College for a short period of time in 1972 and then dropped out. He traveled the world for several years, spending the bulk of his time in India studying Zen Buddhism and seeking spiritual enlightenment.

After his return to Silicon Valley, at the age of 21 he and his high school friend Steve Wozniak founded Apple computers. Jobs, who is widely recognized as a pioneer of the personal computer revolution, went on to serve as chairman and chief executive officer (CEO) of Apple Inc., chairman of Pixar, and founder and CEO of NeXT.

It's not difficult to marvel at the inventions and recognize the influence Jobs has had on thousands of would-be start-up CEOs who seek to emulate his vision for supplying the world with gadgets they didn't know they needed.

Jobs summed it up this way:

> Some people say, "Give the customers what they want." But that's not my approach. Our job is to figure out what they're going

to want before they do. I think Henry Ford
once said, "If I'd asked customers what
they wanted, they would have told me, 'A
faster horse!'" People don't know what they
want until you show it to them. That's why
I never rely on market research. Our task is
to read things that are not yet on the page.

Pharma/Biotech

As in the electronics industry, the San Francisco Bay
Area has become one of the two major centers for biotechnology in the country, Boston/Cambridge being the
other.

In 1973, Stanford's Stanley Cohen and the University
of California San Francisco's Herbert Boyer developed
a practical technique for producing recombinant DNA,
which was the breakthrough that opened the possibil-
ity of using genetic engineering to diagnose and combat
disease. They founded Genentech to further that exploration and, in turn, to commercialize their discovery.

Further, in 1979, the company developed synthetic
insulin, which was a huge breakthrough after decades
pharmacological dependence on Eli Lilly's process of har-
vesting the drug from cow and pig pancreases.

Genentech became the first biotech company to go
public. Its 1980 initial public offering triggered huge public and investor interest in the biotechnology industry.

The bulk of Genentech's organization in Silicon
Valley was merged with pharmaceutical giant Hoffman-
LaRoche in 1990, and Roche acquired a majority interest

in 2009. Nevertheless, Genentech remains the anchor of the Bay Area biotech cluster, employing more than 3,500 at its headquarters and chief manufacturing facility in South San Francisco.

In addition, former Genentech employees have started more than 30 local spin-offs, which account for an additional 3,700 jobs in the area.

The Bay Area benefits from an impressive combination of intellectual and financial capital. Biotech firms have spun off from each of the region's three major research institutions (Stanford, Berkeley, and the University of California at San Francisco). Additionally, Silicon Valley continues to have the largest concentration of venture capital investors in the world, including the greatest number of highly active biotech investors.

As biotechnology gained prominence among investors, the San Francisco Bay Area has emerged as a hotbed of biotech innovation. Seventy biotech firms, including Genentech, Amgen, and Exelixis, make their home within a two-square mile area in South San Francisco. Novartis, Actelion, and Roche also have their headquarters in the Bay Area.

In the relatively short time since Intel first manufactured its programmable computer chip in the late 1960s, innovation drawing on electronic tech has continued to contribute to pharma tech developments, as with cloud biology, computational medicine, and therapeutics.

Twist Bioscience, for example, developed a storage system which converts the 1's and 0's of digital data into the four letters of synthetic DNA. A single body's DNA can store as much data as 150,000 electronic data centers; the system uses much less electrical power to run, and is projected to last 100,000 years.

Xsensio created its Lab-on-Skin nanowearable devices that exploit biochemical information on the skin's surface. QGel designs customized in-vitro cellular microenvironments for cancer drug screening.

Venture Capital

Venture capital (VC) includes both personal and institutional investment funding that supports the developments of new technologies, particularly computer and pharmaceutical tech. Money is a major motor in San Francisco Bay Area innovation. VC firms organize wealthy investors who seek opportunities as angel investors and later stage funders.

In a 2016 *Harvard Business Review* article, "The Reason Silicon Valley Beat Out Boston for VC Dominance," Anil Gupta and Haiyan Wang reviewed the emergence of Silicon Valley as the nation's dominant force in VC investing.

They reference AnnaLee Saxenian's identification of major differentiators, from cultural factors to state-level policies, and they note how California's prohibition of non-compete covenants supports the region's social and technical interdependencies.

They add three specific factors within the VC arc that supported the Bay Area's predominance:

- The increasing importance of digital technology in almost all industries, and Silicon Valley's dominance in that arena

- Silicon Valley's expertise in building structures that enable start-up and smaller companies to scale up quickly and efficiently, again drawn from experience in the IT world
- The availability of large amounts of private capital in the Bay Area, enabling new ventures to raise large sums of venture funding without needing to go public before they are ready

It's been noted that San Francisco values risk-taking and accepts failures in the process. An informal operating rule of thumb has been that if a VC investment fund backs ten new enterprises, the fund expects to break even if just one in ten succeeds, and the fund and its investors do very well when three out of ten survive to a mature stage for acquisition or for an initial public offering.

Many of the venture capitalists in the Bay Area are people who had previously earned significant wealth in a start-up technology company that grew to major success.

Hiten Shah, for example, started on the internet by founding an internet marketing consultancy, ACS. He co-founded Space Pencil Inc. in 2008 and serves as its president and chief executive officer.

Shah is also the founder and chief executive officer of KissMetrics, where he builds data-driven solutions to help online businesses make better business decisions. He co-founded Crazy Egg & Quick Sprout, an analytics tool that visualizes the user experience on a website. In addition, he serves as a venture advisor at 15Five, Inc., and Lean Startup Machine Inc, and as a general business development advisor to nearly a dozen other companies.

A more widely known investor is Apple co-founder Steve Wozniak, whose focus after Apple has been on venture capital investments in new technology ventures. He is a co-founder of the recently launched blockchain-focused venture capital fund EQUI Global.

More Secrets of Silicon Valley's Success

Why do start-up entrepreneurs want to be in San Francisco and the Bay Area even though rent is cheaper anywhere else in the country? What is it about these few square miles that set it apart from the entire world?

Factors noted above include the reliance on risk-taking and dense social networks and partnerships; the presence of money to support start-ups; open labor markets; a willingness to take risks, and to fail; and a readiness to come out of failures to make new starts drawing upon the lessons of those failures.

There are several additional factors rooted in San Francisco values that contribute to the region's successes.

The area's educational riches, including Stanford University, the University of California at Berkeley, and the University of California San Francisco, effectively present developmental laboratories for the exploration of new technologies.

A pattern was set early on, back in the 1920s and '30s, when Stanford recruited a number of accomplished faculty members from the East Coast — people like Fred Terman. An electronics researcher who came out to

California from MIT, Terman encouraged his students to do research and to create; then, he added actively encouraging and supporting them in taking their developing technologies out to the industrial marketplace.

David Hewlett and William Packard were two of Terman's students. Their first focus was on oscillators, devices that convert direct current to alternating current. Electronic audio-oscillators, which would replace vacuum-tube-based devices, came to include applications in radio and television transmitters, the now very familiar sounds produced by beepers and video games, and the internal clocks in computers; they also had military applications. Hewlett and Packard sold their audio oscillators to the Disney corporation; the income would enable them to develop Hewlett-Packard, now one of the world's major computer companies.

The Bay Area mindset supports those wanting to create a new company. The area pioneered many cooperative organizations, sometimes called "incubators," to help young entrepreneurs get started with the business side of things. In addition to moral and physical support, there is a lot of money floating around just looking to invest in the next big thing...or even small thing...or anything the venture capital people think will sell, whether it is a physical project, software, or service.

With all these pieces and parts of an opportunity in a cauldron that encourages combining the right talent, connections, and skills, it may be only a matter of time before there's yet another new and successful company to add to the list.

Another not-so-secret factor in the success of Silicon Valley is San Francisco's historic international ties and continuing global interactions, including welcoming attitudes toward immigrants, enabling the companies and the community to draw upon the strengths of a diverse population. This contrasts with immigration and globalization fears in several other parts of the United States.

Back in 2008, the Bay Area Council poll revealed that, by a huge majority, local residents — 88% of them — endorsed the fast speeding up in global trade, as well as economic and cultural connections between the Bay Area with other countries.

This international perspective continues. As of March 1, 2020, the Bay Area Council Economic Institute and the Los Angeles Area Chamber of Commerce jointly own TradePort, a premier online resource for comprehensive information about the "how-to" aspects of importing and exporting. TradePort also supports California's trade promotion service, the first such statewide promotional effort in the country.

This world-focused enthusiasm, at least in part, can be related to the fact that many Bay Area residents are migrants themselves. Twenty-seven percent of residents in the region's nine counties were born outside the United States, in contrast to 13% nationwide. Thirty-nine percent of residents in San Jose and 31% of residents of San Francisco speak both English and at least one other language at home, which is also twice the national average, reflecting the richness of the vast international talent pool to be found within the Bay Area's melting pot society.

Of all new entrepreneurs in 2016, 29.5% were immigrants.

Shahin Shadfar's career gives one illustration of such immigrant talent. He was born in Tehran, Iran, and educated in Paris and then at Georgia Tech.

A migrant to San Francisco's South of Market tech hub, via Texas, Shadfar developed web and video conferencing applications, and then the mobile app Zurf. He was one of a number of creatively talented people who became part of the community in the Bay Area with Middle Eastern origins.

Trisha Roy, who is living out her dream in Silicon Valley, hails from India. She migrated to the United States with a determination to live a better life. She earned an MBA degree at the University of Arizona and moved to the Bay Area, where she discovered that the best-paying jobs were in tech.

In her native country, Roy had never had any experience with technology, as women were not given the opportunity of employment in the field of engineering. After arriving in the Bay Area, she taught herself the basics in coding in order to become competitive, and she was successful in gaining employment at eBay. She worked her way up to attain the position of a senior product manager, and then she moved out on her own.

Many tech start-ups have been seen as disruptive to established financial markets, with Craigslist, Lyft, and Airbnb as three well-known examples. Having that same perspective, Roy developed a company that leverages technology in the creation of custom home décor. She summarized her approach: "We are questioning the obvious and disrupting traditional retail."

For those whose worldview would prefer that these talented immigrants not come to the States, you might consider asking: Do we want the best and the brightest from around the world working on our side, or for some other side? Historically, for example, there were the significant contributions made to America and the world by scientists who came here instead of staying in Hitler's Nazi Germany in the 1930s. Two among many were German-born Albert Einstein, with his seminal work in physics, and Austro-Hungarian Erwin Chargaff, whose biochemical studies led us to the double helix structure of DNA.

Company development and growth get boosted in the Silicon Valley area because the majority of start-up investors and venture capital firms provide an immense amount of support, mentorship, guidance, and connections, above and beyond just a financial investment, to their portfolio companies. The broad availability of such support means that aligning with the right investor, one that provides mentoring and connections, becomes a key decision in seeking funding options.

There is important access to positive business conveniences in the Bay Area. The area offers no end of comforts such as hotels, world-class restaurants, sports teams, and a lot of entertainment options to impress potential investors.

Past regional success stories also provide inspiration...from the earlier successes of the gold and silver miners, to the current successful initial public offerings of many start-ups. Potential Bay Area companies inhale those tales, hoping to have the same experience. People want to be surrounded by success and to see themselves in the same league, whether as an entrepreneur or investor. For those hoping to walk the same path as Google, Apple, or Facebook, the stories never end. Yet each story has its own path, and there is a community of hopefuls that will gladly try to replicate those experiences. It makes the trip less lonely.

While it may seem counterintuitive, stories of past entrepreneurial failures can provide encouragement along with the shining Silicon Valley success stories.

Heitor Martins, Yran Bartolomeu Dias, and Somesh Khanna are three highly respected business experts who conducted in-depth interviews with 50 Silicon Valley entrepreneurs in large, midsize, and start-up companies to study factors that transformed the area into an unbelievable success. They succeeded in discovering that the daily fortitude to attain success, in spite of near-continuous failures, is totally universal among entrepreneurs operating in the valley.

Martins, Bartolomeu Dias, and Khanna reported their findings in the *Harvard Business Review*:

> The kind of innovation that creates new markets always goes against the grain...We found people at all levels to be especially levelheaded about failure and comfortable with the inherent messiness of experimentation. The magic for them is not

something's initial lightbulb moment but
the commitment to assessing, refining, and
reintroducing the systems that will make
the thing work.

The authors found corporate cultures and management styles predominant in organizations where teams
self-organize; where people from various functions often
come together to work on specific projects; and where
good ideas gain momentum organically by attracting talent from around the business.

Managers act more as enablers and connectors, providing regular feedback and tracking progress. Formal
organizational hierarchies and belabored consensus-
building processes are seen as artificial constraints that
create waste and dampen motivation. The most innovative companies set clear expectations around goals and
investment risk but let employees define the best way to
meet them. The focus is on outcomes, on the successful
execution of good ideas in a real-world marketplace.

Yet another aspect of the differences between Bay
Area tech companies and more traditional companies
has to do with what the company brings to the marketplace. Historically, an enterprise would produce tangible items, ranging from cars to clothing to carrot juice.
Measures of success were found in efficiently managing
production schedules and costs, and in increasing the
number of items sold.

In contrast, in Silicon Valley, small business consultant and author Larry Alton notes, "a growing number of
technology startups don't even build physical products

for their customers." Industry jargon refers to this as the difference between a "product," such as the tangible items just named, and a "platform."

Jonathan Clark, who runs a private stock investment firm, explains that platforms are "structures that allow multiple products to be built within the same technical framework," and that "companies invest in platforms in the hope that future products can be developed faster and cheaper, than if they built them stand-alone."

Clark points out different areas of activity, such as the online retail framework of Amazon, the social media framework of Facebook, and the online micropayment framework that is Apple iTunes. Amazon, he notes, "built a retail platform that gathered huge amounts of data on how people buy things online. They used this knowledge to extend the platform to sell more and different things." The expansion of the gig economy ride services like Lyft and Uber to include meal deliveries, obvious after the fact, illustrates the extension of their original platform.

Alton explains that a platform's value is determined by the users that populate it, and by its ability to easily be morphed into something else down the road that better fits user needs.

By and large, the myth and matching reality that is Silicon Valley has served as a model for communities around the world seeking to emulate its success. One place for them to start is to understand and then adopt and emulate San Francisco's values.

Take Action

1. **Risk-taking.** Both in your personal life and your political life, be willing to take reasonable risks to reach for goals and accomplishments, and vote to elect others with that same mindset.

2. **Failure.** Even the best of us fail. Often. Consider professional sports. A shooting average of 50% is considered good in basketball; a batting average of 33% is good in baseball; and in professional soccer games, a good shot-to-score ratio is between 40 and 60%. Look at how those who seek to lead us handle their failures — hopefully, with a combination of grace and the readiness to be back up and moving forward again toward desired goals.

3. **Collective learning and partnerships.** The Silicon Valley approach to sharing information and to open organizational structures provides a successful model. Assess whether those you consider supporting accomplish their (and your) goals by working effectively with other people.

4. **Platforms.** Support people who are capable of building solutions that can be scaled upward, and that can be applied to related issues. That is, seek those who conceptualize solutions with a platform mentality.

5. **Incubators.** Evaluate whether people are willing to learn from others and who also, in turn, mentor and teach others, so that we build on the strengths of those who have come before and pass on our wisdom to those coming next.

CHAPTER 4

How San Francisco Celebrates Love and Families in All Their Diversity

Yes, be afraid of the "gay agenda." We ARE coming for your children. And we are going to make them ... TOLERANT.

— *San Francisco Gay Men's Chorus*

In Massachusetts, you can be anyone you want to be...as long as you do it in your own home...behind closed doors...and you don't talk about it in public. In San Francisco, you can be anyone you want to be...and you can do so out loud and in public...and there are probably three support groups for it.

— *A Bay Area transplant from the East Coast*

Sexuality is an issue that touches every person alive. Our conception is a sexual act, and most societies have rules or norms that set boundaries on sexual behavior. The linking of two people together through marriage is found in societies across the globe. Incest is a common taboo. Human bodies mature to enable sexual relations, and our hormones drive the desire for sexuality — more or less strongly — in most all of us. And our values governing sexual behavior are deeply embedded in us, by our societal groups, and particularly by our religious groups, from a very young age.

The right for all people to express their sexuality as they choose, as long as it is consensual, is an important value in the San Francisco Bay Area.

Evolving Sexual Values

We can often trace a country's shifting values through its media. America's viewpoint has changed over the years, moving toward an increasing acceptance of LGBTQ relationships.

Here are three (out of many) examples that reflect the growing acceptance of those dynamics across America:

- In 2005, the movie *Brokeback Mountain* sensitively portrayed the gay relationship between two cow-boys, played by Heath Ledger and Jake Gyllenhaal. It was a box office hit; it was also nominated for eight Oscars and won three of them, including Best Director.
- Jane Fonda and Lily Tomlin star in the Netflix-streaming *Grace and Frankie,* which has been airing since 2015. The women learn that their husbands, played by Martin Sheen and Sam

Waterson, were partners in a law firm who were also romantically involved with each other for 20 years. The couples split, the two men marry, and the two women evolve their own friendship. The show has a strong audience, and has been nominated for five Emmys and has won one Golden Globe Award.

- Jill Soloway's comedy series *Transparent* began airing on Amazon Prime in 2014, when Jeffrey Tambor, playing Morton, the father in the Pfefferman family, announced to his family that he was beginning his transition into the woman Maura. The show won a Golden Globe for Best Series and has had multiple Golden Globe and Emmy nominations. Tambor received 22 major acting award nominations, and he won 13 of them.

Studies and polls also show that same-sex marriage is, happily, an issue where American values have been catching up with San Francisco values.

Both the Pew Research Center and the Gallup Poll have very consistent numbers in polls on the subject. Pew's 2019 report includes:

- Americans opposed same-sex marriage by a margin of 60% to 31% in 2004.
- Support for same-sex marriage has steadily grown over the past 15 years. Polling in 2019 shows that a majority of Americans (61%) support same-sex marriage, while 31% oppose it.

- Among people who are religiously unaffiliated, a solid majority have supported same-sex marriage since 2004, with 79% saying that same-sex couples should be allowed to marry.
- About two-thirds of white mainline Protestants (66%) now support same-sex marriage, as do a similar share of Catholics (61%).
- Support for same-sex marriage among white evangelical Protestants remains lower than it is among other religious groups. However, the share of white evangelical Protestants who support same-sex marriage has grown from 11% in 2004 to 29% today.
- 75% of Democrats and Democratic-leaning independents and 44% of Republicans and Republican leaners favor same-sex marriage.
- 66% of women and 57% of men support same-sex marriage. 62% of whites support same-sex marriage, as do 58% of Hispanics and 51% of blacks.
- The United States is one of 29 countries and jurisdictions allowing gay and lesbian couples to wed.

Gallup reports very similar figures, with 63% of Americans saying same-sex marriage should be legal. When Gallup first polled on the question in 1996, just over a quarter of Americans said it should be legal.

Some religions have labeled same-sex relationships as evil and have tried to export that belief so as to impose it on all of society. The extensive campaign run by the Mormon Church against California's 2008 same-sex marriage referendum is one well-documented example of that.

One counter-position is that marriage and other partnered relationships are a civil issue rather than a religious one.

In San Francisco, the value is that, as human beings, we each and all have the personal freedom to live, to love, and to worship or not worship as we choose. San Francisco values don't impose political or religious bounds on any person's right to express their own humanity, their own sexual identity, and their freedom to love others as they choose. In sum, the ethos is: "I respect your right to worship and to love as you choose, and I similarly expect you to respect mine."

Today, majorities of most groups support gay marriage — with the exception of adults aged 65 and older (47%) and Republicans (44%). And regionally, the South remains the least supportive of same-sex marriages, though a growing majority (57%) now supports it. At least 60% of those polled also say that gay or lesbian relations are morally acceptable.

FiveThirtyEight.com reports similar figures: A majority of black people (52%), Hispanics (61%), and white people (63%) back same-sex marriage. The majority of people in all but six states support it. And even in those six states — Alabama, Louisiana, Mississippi, North Carolina, Tennessee, and West Virginia — only in Alabama are opponents an outright majority. Strangely enough, the headline on this report focused on saying: "Support for Same-Sex Marriage Isn't Unanimous."

Fox News has also recognized reality on this topic. In 2018, the conservative media leader reported: "For the first time in a Fox News poll, a majority says same-sex marriage should be legal." Their figures lag other pollsters, yet even they show 54% of registered voters favor legalizing same-sex marriage, with 35% opposed.

Another note on America's evolving values relates to Harvey Milk, who was the first openly gay elected official in California; he served on the San Francisco Board of Supervisors until his assassination in 1978.

Milk had graduated from officer training and served as a diving officer on a submarine rescue ship during the Korean War. However, after his superiors caught him in a park that was popular with gay men, his sexual orientation was questioned, and he was forced to resign from the US Navy.

In July 2019, Terminal 1 at San Francisco Airport reopened after a major renovation, and it was named the Harvey Milk Terminal. Even more of a smile emerges upon learning that, in December 2019, the navy announced that it is building a ship that is to be named after him.

Milk strongly encouraged gay and lesbian men and women to come out of the closet. His perspective was that once people realize that it is their child, their uncle, their granddaughter, their congregation member at church, or a parent of a kid who plays on the same ball team that their kid plays on, windows of tolerance would open more quickly. He also wanted to see the burden of silence and hiding lifted from the souls of these good people. In 1978, he said,

Gay brothers and sisters, you must come
out. Come out to your parents. I know
that it is hard and will hurt them, but think
about how they will hurt you in the voting
booth! Come out to your relatives. Come
out to your friends, if indeed they are your
friends. Come out to your neighbors, to
your fellow workers, to the people who
work where you eat and shop. Come out
only to the people you know, and who
know you, not to anyone else. But once and
for all, break down the myths. Destroy the
lies and distortions. For your sake. For their
sake.

San Francisco's history of toleration wasn't unblem-
ished. Even though it was illegal in the 1960s to be
cross-dressed in public, members of the cross-dressing
and transgendered communities, including a number of
prostitutes, would come together in the late nights and
early mornings in the Tenderloin, notably at Compton's
Cafeteria on Taylor Street, to socialize, share stories,
and have coffee. It was a tight-knit social setting, whose
members looked out for each other.

While heavy police enforcement of the cross-dressing
ban wasn't the rule, it was known that the police on the
Tenderloin beat made extra money by regularly shaking
down Compton's owners and/or the individuals there,
and, on occasion, roughing them up or hauling them in
for a night in jail.

In August 1966, a police raid, complete with a paddy wagon, arrived at Compton's. One of the patrons, tired of being hassled and manhandled yet again, threw a cup of hot coffee into a cop's face, and an all-out riot began in the shop.

Demonstrations and some further riots for transgender rights were fomented in the summer of 1966, as drag queens and their supporters poured into the streets and fought back with their high heels and heavy bags. There was limited press coverage of these events outside of the Bay Area at that time.

San Francisco values have evolved since 1966 to embrace those who find their gender in question or romantically love someone of the same sex. These values are held high, and there is now much support that the city offers. A number of churches, like the Glide Memorial Methodist Church in San Francisco, were leaders in reaching out to offer support to the transgender community.

In June 1969, similar riots unfolded in New York City's Greenwich Village, in response to a police raid on the gay Stonewall Inn. These better-publicized New York demonstrations are generally portrayed as the major impetus for the public battle for LGBTQ rights in the United States and internationally.

This battle, as with many other social movements in America, flowed from the West Coast to the East Coast, and then to the heartland of the country. In April 1970, Chicago's LGBTQ community organized to fight persecution with pickets and protests in front of the Normandy Inn, where arrests of people dancing with members of the same gender were being made with the charge of "public indecency." The protesters' banners and leaflets called for "the right to dance any tempo, any style." Within two weeks, the club's owners were able to get a license for same-sex dancing.

While two-thirds of mainline Protestants now support same-sex marriage, it is still an issue for some. The United Methodist Church claims to allow for a wide range of theological and political beliefs, and its broad membership includes former president George W. Bush, former attorney general Jeff Sessions, Senator Elizabeth Warren, and former secretary of state Hillary Clinton.

In 2019, following extensive discussion and despite pressure from many of its members, the United Methodist Church leadership voted to continue its bans on same-sex marriages and on openly LGBTQ people serving as clergy. On November 6, 2019, five bishops representing the Western Jurisdiction of the United Methodist Church released a statement in support of LGBTQ clergy. There is a strong sense that the church may split into two different organizations, and a vote on such a possible split was calendared for May 2020.

In Philadelphia, home of Independence Hall, where the Constitution was signed and the Liberty Bell rung, a United Methodist Church booth was a sponsor at Philadelphia's 2019 LGBTQ Pride celebration. Their table featured a sign that read: "Please accept this apology from the United Methodist Church."

One Pride Fair attendee approached the UMC booth in order to inquire about the sign. He reported that a member of the Church, who was sitting at the booth, greeted him as follows:

> Hello. If you have ever been harmed by the United Methodist Church's stance on homosexuality, we would like the opportunity to apologize. Please accept our apology for the harm we have caused to LGBT members of our congregation. We failed to accept you as a perfect creation of God. We are ashamed of the damage we have caused to your community and to ourselves and we hope you will forgive us.

Back on the other side of the country, the San Jose probation department announced their support of their city's 2019 Pride parade with this statement: "Over the last 7 years, Probation and the County has made great strides in increasing our acceptance, understanding, support and advocacy for our LGBTQIA clients, staff and community."

The Missouri Older Adult Alliance has now been established, as a partnership among SAGE of PROMO Fund, the St. Louis City Area Agency on Aging, Aging Ahead, and Missouri's Department of Health and Senior Services, to ensure competent care for older LGBT people.

Similarly, the San Francisco Bay Area's Santa Clara County, the first county in the nation to have every city in it designated as an Age-Friendly City, is currently conducting a study on the status of the LGBTQ senior community's needs.

One hallmark of the San Francisco Bay Area is an abiding respect for individual rights and individual choices, for the right to live and express one's own lifestyle, whatever that might be, without fear of judgment or constraints, so long as those choices are not forced on others.

Growing Up Gay

Studies show that most people who identify as gay and lesbian know this at an early age. Our own research supports this: everyone we interviewed said they had feelings of being different or having attraction to the same gender before the age of ten.

Those same-sex couples interviewed for this book grew up in a wide range of rural, suburban, and urban communities with straight parents. Some families were understanding and supportive, but most were not. We look at four people who found their way to acceptance in the San Francisco Bay area LGBT community.

Marvin Burrows and William Sweenor

Marvin Burrows has known that he was gay since he was eight years old. He grew up in a rural community outside of Flint, Michigan. His best friend was his male cousin; they confided in each other and compared notes about different boys they knew.

"I knew I was different, a sissy, and the kids at my school treated me differently," Burrows said. "My cousin met and had experiences with boys, and we would compare boyfriends and stuff."

His parents began suspecting an odd relationship between Marvin and his cousin and discouraged the friendship between the boys by limiting their communication and visits. Marvin missed his "best friend" cousin's conversations, and he became more isolated.

Finally, feeling very much alone, Burrows walked from his home to the family barn, tossed a rope around a beam, fashioned a knot, and put his head through the loop.

He jumped off a set of stairs and hung in the air for what seemed like hours. The knot slipped, and Burrows crashed to the floor, choking and gasping for air.

He lay there, staring up at nothing, motionless. Gradually images in the barn became clear. Rafters, stairs, dust balls sharpened into view, and Burrows realized, with regret, he wasn't dead.

No one came looking for him, so after an hour or so, he dragged himself back into the house, went into his room, and covered himself with the blankets on his bed.

When Burrows's mother found him, she knew why her son tried to kill himself; she looked into having him committed to an institution but stopped short of going through with it.

"My mother was more accepting than my stepfather. He wouldn't talk to me," Burrows said. "They wanted to cure me, so they sent me to a psychiatrist. If it were not for that psychiatrist helping me to accept who I am, I don't know what kind of life I would have or even if I'd have a life."

Several years later, Burrows met William Sweenor, who would become his life partner. They knew they needed to leave Flint and live somewhere else that would be more accepting of who they were.

They explored San Francisco and moved to the Bay Area in 1960. Sweenor, who had worked for General Motors in Michigan, transitioned to a supervisory role in a glass-manufacturing plant. Burrows found a sales position, and then worked as a sales manager for a large retail company; he also volunteered at a senior center and for Meals on Wheels.

"I wish all those people who were so critical could see me now. My relationship lasted longer than all their marriages put together," Burrows said. He and Sweenor had been together for 51 years when Sweenor died in 2002.

Their relationship was like any other couple who are together for a long time, he said.

Discrimination and lack of understanding toward homosexual children continues to be a major cause of suicides and suicide attempts among gay adolescent and teenage children.

According to the findings of an October 2018 Rutgers University study, sexual minority youth were more than three times as likely to attempt suicide as their heterosexual peers; among them, transgender youth were at highest risk, nearly six times as likely to attempt suicide as heterosexual peers.

Burrows and Sweenor are illustrative of many nontraditional couples who choose to move to the Bay Area in order to find a community where family and personal values are inclusive, where a range of expressions of gender and broad definitions of family are part of the fabric.

The San Francisco Bay Area has earned its reputation for respecting individual rights, individual choices, and the right to live and express one's own lifestyle without fear of the judgment or constraints of others. Interviews with people from South America, Europe, Asia, and Africa generate consistent descriptions of San Francisco as a "live and let live" society, as a community of individualists, bohemians, and gay rights activists who want to be free to make their own personal choices of friends, partners, and spouses.

Frank Howell and John Wise

Frank Howell left Redbluff, California, a town located 131 miles north of Sacramento in California's Central Valley, when he was 20 years old, to escape the tyranny of small-town isolation and disapproval. He began to realize he was gay in junior high school, when he wrote a romantic novel about a group of young boys who ran away to live together and form their own family together as lovers. His parents found the novel, and they were alarmed at the nature of book's content with respect to the male characters' obvious affection for one another. They took Howell to the Langley Porter Psychiatric Institute at the University of California San Francisco Medical Center to have him evaluated for a psychiatric disorder.

Howell said the psychiatrists tested him extensively with interviews, written preference exams, and image identification. They came up with nothing. "They had no diagnosis and called it off," he said. His parents took him home and the issue was never discussed again.

They just buried the entire incident, but after a while, they went for counseling as the "parents of a gay child." His mother remained indifferent, neither hostile nor loving, for a long time. His father, however, was distant and disapproving, telling his son he would be a lonely old man with no friends.

Howell remembers that he didn't suffer from verbal or physical abuse from other kids or adults. Rather, it was more that no one acknowledged his existence. His parents disapproved of his choices, and the other kids at school locked him out of groups and activities. He felt very much alone in the world.

Two years after he graduated from high school, Howell met his life partner, John Wise. They were together for 25 years, until Wise died in 1998.

After they met and became a couple, the two came to San Francisco for a weekend vacation. They attended a Sunday service at the Glide Memorial Church. "We thought it was amazing and daring that the ministers were counseling with what people called 'sexual perverts,'" Howell recalled. "Everyone was accepted and respected for who they were, not for who someone else thought they should be."

They knew they had found where they wanted to settle down. They moved to the Bay Area, where Howell got his master's degree in library science, and then worked at the Hayward library in Hayward, California, a suburban community 35 miles southeast of San Francisco in the East Bay.

Marriage Equality

Burrows, Sweenor, Howell, and Wise each wanted to be more than just part of "a gay couple."

Taking their respective relationships as seriously as any other couple in love, they wanted to make the commitment to each other that is formalized by marriage. It was important to have their bonds recognized by their families and friends, so they planned wedding ceremonies and invited everyone in their lives to join with them in a celebration of their relationship. Although the state or federal governments at the time did not recognize same-sex marriage, it didn't matter. Each couple wanted a wedding ceremony, legal or not, to tell their communities and the world they were committed to each other for life.

"We matter as a family, just like any other," said Burrows.

Same-sex couples were seeking the same recognition of their relationships as hetero couples. Legalizing same-sex marriage had become a hotly contested issue all over the country. Finally, on June 26, 2015, the US Supreme Court ruled, in *Obergefell v. Hodges*, that state-level bans on same-sex marriage are unconstitutional. The court ruled that the denial of marriage licenses to same-sex couples and the refusal to recognize those marriages performed in other jurisdictions violates the "due process" and the "equal protection" clauses of the 14th Amendment of the US Constitution.

The ruling overturned a 1972 precedent, *Baker v. Nelson*. Just prior to the Supreme Court's ruling in 2015,

some form of same-sex marriage or domestic partnership had become legal in 38 US jurisdictions.

Before the ruling, California law sought to give registered domestic partners the same responsibilities and
rights as married couples. Federal law, however, did not.
Committed same-sex couples were not eligible for Social
Security benefits, immigration privileges, or the marriage
exemptions allowed in federal estate, transfer, or gift
taxes.

The arguments for same-gender marriages had
gained steam, piecemeal, across the country. After
taking office in February 2004, San Francisco mayor
Gavin Newsom took a gutsy stand, openly challenging
California license law by allowing same-sex couples to
receive marriage licenses and get married.

Newsom made the decision to allow the full rights of
marriage after hearing President Bush oppose it during
his State of the Union Address on January 20, 2004. At
that time, as has been noted, Pew Research Center polling showed that Americans opposed same-sex marriage
by a margin of 60% to 31%.

"This is about bringing people together," Newsom
said. He directed his chief of staff to prepare the city
for an onslaught of gay and lesbian couples who would
apply for marriage licenses. Over two thousand gay and
lesbian couples applied the first day.

Previously, gay and lesbian couples had been able to
register as domestic partners in California. Couples who
registered were eligible for many of the same state rights
as heterosexual married couples, but only in the state of

California. The rights of civil unions did not transfer from state to state as marriage does.

Of the 1,138 federal rights that came with marriage, but were not extended to gay couples, one of the most devastating to gay couples was the loss of a survivor's spousal rights when one member of the couple died.

Bill Sweenor died from a heart attack after the couple had lived together for 51 years, had bought a home together, and had shared all of the things that any long-time married couple does. Marvin Burrows was treated by the system as nothing more than a casual friend. He lost the health insurance he'd had as Bill's domestic partner, and he was denied Sweenor's spousal pension and Social Security benefits.

Burrows could not afford the mortgage on the home they had lived in for 30 years, and his own Social Security payment would barely cover his new health insurance costs, leaving nothing for food and housing. In one week, Burrows lost the love of his life and was facing homelessness.

Burrows petitioned Sweenor's union for his pension. The petition was denied. Under Sweenor's union rules, while surviving spouses continued to receive health insurance benefits, domestic partners of union members lost their benefits once their domestic partner died.

Several years later, the union changed their policy to treat survivors of same-sex domestic partnerships the same as married survivors.

Burrows also encountered a problem at the mortuary where Sweenor's body was sent: they would not cremate him at Burrow's request, refusing to accept domestic partner Burrows as the next of kin legally entitled to make such decisions. Burrows had to have Sweenor's body moved to another, more accepting, crematorium.

Other frequent insults and indignities for same-sex couples occurred when a partner in a long-term gay relationship would be refused visitation at hospitals by previously distant and disapproving family members, who swooped in and excluded the mates from being with their dying loved ones, and then raided the assets left behind as well.

Marriage as a Civil Rights Issue

Same-sex marriage is a civil rights issue. In the words of Theodore B. Olson, quoted from a *Newsweek* article:

> Legalizing same-sex marriage would also be a recognition of basic American principles, and would represent the culmination of our nation's commitment to equal rights.

Olsen, who had served as US solicitor general under President George W. Bush, wrote that marriage is a civil issue, not a religious one, that it represents a civil contract between people, just as in business. As he stressed, whether a religion condones same-sex marriage or not, religion is not the law of the land and has no place in regulating a civil contract that is recognized for most of its citizens.

Olson, a political conservative, also declared: "Same-sex marriage is the last major civil-rights milestone yet to be surpassed in our two-century struggle to attain the goals we set for this nation at its formation."

Fortunately, the law eventually changed, and equality for all is now the law of the land and the center of our political and legal convictions. Whether a person is a liberal or a conservative, these civil rights began as the revolutionary concept that our nation was founded upon.

Between February 11 and March 11, 2004, more than three thousand couples took advantage of the short window that Mayor Gavin Newsom had opened.

The legal dispute over the issuance of marriage licenses to same-sex couples found its way to the California Supreme Court in 2008. Lesbian couple Diane Sabin and Jewell Gomez had been asked to participate and become plaintiffs in a lawsuit against the state. They agreed primarily for the political statement it would make. They won their case in June 2008 but still had no burning personal interest in getting married.

The court's decision was taken to a statewide public constitutional referendum in November 2008. Titled "Proposition 8," the proposal was also widely known as "Proposition Hate"—it succeeded in barring same-sex marriages in California. That status lasted until June 2013, when Proposition 8 was overturned as unconstitutional.

With the looming 2008 vote on Proposition 8, Sabin and Gomez finally decided to marry, scheduling their ceremony the weekend before the Prop. 8 votes.

"Looking out at the hugely varied spectrum of people assembled for our wedding in the San Francisco public library we could see why a public union was important—it created community," said Gomez. "We are very fortunate we have love. The world would be a better place if more people had love."

The window was then closed, by legal and electoral challenges, and battles were fought on the issue, culminating in the 2015 US Supreme Court Ruling in support of same-sex marriage.

In that ruling, Justice Anthony Kennedy's majority opinion included:

> Rising from the most basic human needs, marriage is essential to our most profound hopes and aspirations.

> The centrality of marriage to the human condition makes it unsurprising that the institution has existed for millennia and across civilizations.

> Since the dawn of history, marriage has transformed strangers into relatives, binding families and societies together.

> Confucius taught us that marriage lies at the foundation of government.

> This wisdom was echoed centuries later and half a world away by Cicero, who wrote, 'The first bond of society is marriage; next, children; and then the family.'

No union is more profound than marriage,
for it embodies the highest ideals of love,
fidelity, devotion, sacrifice, and family.

Integrity versus Hypocrisy

San Francisco Bay Area people, just like those in most other parts of the country, value integrity and resent hypocrisy. Nowhere, it seems, does hypocrisy surface more than in the sexual arenas. And there are knowing nods and smirks in those cases in which some legislators, and some religious leaders, who strongly supported anti-LGBTQ legislation, are then found participating in the very same behavior in their private lives.

The list of GOP lawmakers who voted against LGBTQ legislation while publicly railing against some fictitious gay agendas and were then found to act very differently in private is long. Our problem, of course, is not with what they did, but rather with the hypocrisy underlying their attacks. This extensive and yet abbreviated list reflects back to Harvey Milk's belief that if all gay people simply came out, the extent of this behavior in human beings would be more fully and adequately recognized and more easily accepted.

GOP Speaker of the House from 1999 to 2007, Dennis Hastert was well-known for his anti-gay stands and his vocal "family values" position. At his 2016 sentencing hearing, Hastert admitted that he had sexually abused boys during his years as a high school wrestling coach; he had paid $1.7 million out of $3.5 million in promised hush money across several decades to keep that behavior secret.

Ohio GOP lawmaker Wes Goodman, who touted family values, his Christian faith, and anti-LGBT views, resigned after being caught having sex with a man in his office. Goodman is married to a woman who is the assistant director of the annual March for Life anti-abortion rally.

Alabama attorney general Troy King, who sought to ban the sale of sex toys in the state, called homosexuality "the downfall of society" in a 1992 op-ed about a college LGBT group. In 2008, it was reported that he was caught by his wife in bed with a male aide.

Washington State representative Richard Curtis, who consistently voted against same-sex domestic partnerships and against an anti-discrimination law protecting gay people, was outed by a male escort who had been blackmailing him and threatening to tell his wife about their trysts.

From 2001 to 2005, Ed Schrock served as US Representative for Virginia's Second Congressional District. He stood 100 percent against gay rights. He dropped plans for reelection, though, when a tape of him soliciting sex with men on a gay chat line surfaced.

Maryland congressman Robert Bauman preached about the collapse of American morality and founded numerous conservative organizations, including the Young Americans for Freedom and the American Conservative Union. He was arrested for attempting to solicit sex from a 16-year-old male prostitute.

The 1996 Defense of Marriage Act (DOMA) defined marriage as the union of one man and one woman. It allowed states to refuse to recognize same-sex marriages granted under the laws of other states and prohibited married same-sex couples from collecting federal benefits. DOMA, passed by the Republican-controlled 104th Congress, was signed into law by Democratic President Bill Clinton. It is duly noted that Clinton's sexual behavior went well beyond his marriage to one woman.

Republican congressman Mark Foley served in the House from 1995 until 2006, where he voted for the Defense of Marriage Act. His downfall came when it was found out that he had been sexting with two male pages, ages 16 and 18 — and, after they reached legal age, reportedly having sex with them.

Bob Allen was a married Florida state representative who voted against gay rights legislation 90% of the time. His "Bathroomgate" was his arrest for offering a male undercover cop $20 in a restroom for oral sex.

In 2011, Republican mayor Chris Myers of Medford, New Jersey, a married, pro-life, anti-marriage-equality politician, was accused of having sex with a male prostitute in a California hotel. The escort went public because Myers had paid him $500, but reneged on a car and other gifts he promised.

Phil Hinkle, a member of the Indiana House of Representatives who voted for a constitutional amendment banning same-sex marriage, likely did not have marriage on his mind when he asked an 18-year-old male he met on Craigslist up to his hotel room. When the young man realized that he had been invited under false pretenses, he changed his mind about the encounter. Hinkle tried to pay him off, but word got out. Hinkle refused to admit he was gay but declined to seek reelection.

Bruce Barclay, chairman of Pennsylvania's Cumberland County Board of Commissioners, was described as a "rising star" in Republican politics. He was very outspoken about his belief that homosexuality was a sin, but he was then caught with hundreds of tapes of him having sex with male prostitutes.

Idaho Republican senator Larry Craig's "Bathroomgate" moment came with his arrest for solicitation of a cop in an airport bathroom. On his arrest, Craig declared that he adopted "a wide stance when going to the bathroom," adding that he may have inadvertently touched the foot of the arresting officer.

After Randy Boehning, a member of the North Dakota House of Representatives, voted against gay rights, he was outed on Grindr, the self-proclaimed world's largest social networking app for gay, bi, trans, and queer people, with explicit photos and messages.

Married Republican Oklahoma state senator Ralph Shortey was caught in a motel room with a 17-year-old boy to whom he had offered money for sex. The boy's father called police. Shortey was arrested. An FBI investigation found that Shortey had contacted numerous young men on Craigslist to exchange pornography. Shortey pleaded guilty to the child-sex trafficking charge.

Vice President Mike Pence has been criticized strongly by members of the LGBTQ community for stances he has taken that negatively impact that community. He sometimes attributes those positions to his religion.

Pete Buttigieg, the former mayor of South Bend, Indiana, was one of the candidates running for the 2020 Democratic nomination for the Presidency. He is openly gay, he is married to his husband, and he is an active member of the Episcopal Church. Mayor Pete expressed his issue with Vice President Pence with two widely quoted statements:

> The vice president is entitled to his religious beliefs. My problem is when those religious beliefs are used as an excuse to harm other people.

> If me being gay was a choice, it was a choice that was made far, far above my pay grade. And that's the thing I wish the Mike Pences of the world would understand. That if you got a problem with who I am, your problem is not with me — your quarrel, sir, is with my creator.

In a public forum, a question was posed to Senator Elizabeth Warren about how she would respond to someone who said that his faith teaches him that a marriage is between one man and one woman. Her response, which quickly went viral on the internet, was brief and to the point: that she would suggest that he just marry one woman. "I'm cool with that," she said, clearly signaling that she believes in allowing him to act on his beliefs, and in turn allowing others to follow their respective beliefs.

It's clear there are conflicting views regarding LGBTQ issues and the conservative agenda. It is doubtful that personal feelings will change with new laws. However, while people are entitled to have their opinions, as a society, we need to let others live their life the way they want to, as long as they don't try to impose their beliefs on others. And our laws need to reflect that.

Remember the mantra: live and let live.

Take Action

1. **Personal freedom of expression.** Each of us has the right to be our own honest selves, and to love and live with those we choose. Separate and vote out those who seek to limit these personal freedoms. Vote out those who attack or bully others for who they are. Vote in, instead, those who support the individual rights and protections of all of us.

2. **Societal freedom of expression.** We need a free press to continue the expression of and exploration of the range of our interests. Recent attacks on the press have moved from traditional political complaints of being misquoted to out-and-out attacks on the press and its reporters. Do not support those whose speeches and political actions identify the press as the enemy, particularly because our continuation as a democracy requires a free press.

3. **The children.** For most of us, going into and through puberty had its difficulties. For children who feel different, who need to explore their possible LGBTQ identities, the problems are multiplied. These children need love and support from their parents, and caring within their communities. Support candidates, from school boards to the presidency, who support the kids. Exile from office and from power in our communities those who seek to forcibly change the sexual identity of our children, teens, and young adults as they navigate these perilous waters.

4. **Integrity.** Is your elected official honest? Lies may seem to be a norm in politics, but are they ever ethically defensible? Examine the verbal honesty and the behavioral honesty of those on the ballot. Does their behavior match their words? Do they promise you a tax cut but give it instead to very rich individuals and corporations? Do they attack people for behaving just as they themselves secretly behave? Regardless of your political affiliation, demand that there be truth in politics from anyone who's asking for your vote.

CHAPTER 5

San Francisco Supports Our Troops

In his song titled "San Francisco (Be Sure to Wear Flowers in Your Hair)" John Phillips tells us that "you're gonna meet some gentle people there." And in Dionne Warwick's song "Do you know the way to San Jose" she tells us she is "going back to find some peace of mind."

There is always inequity in life. Some men are killed in a war, and some men are wounded, and some men are stationed in the Antarctic and some are stationed in San Francisco. It's very hard in military or personal life to assure complete equality. Life is unfair.

— *President John F. Kennedy, 1962*

Blind obedience to authority is neither an American nor a San Francisco value.

As shall be shown in detail, the Bay Area has long supported our troops, and continues to do so, with a major emphasis these days on rehabilitation and rehousing for American veterans.

At the same time, the Bay Area has shown leadership in examining when military action is, and when it may not be, in the best interests of the nation.

In Congress

Barbara Lee represents California's 13th Electoral District in Congress, an area that includes Oakland and surrounding East Bay cities. In 2001, she was the only one out of 431 members of the House and 100 members of the Senate to vote against the Authorization for Use of Military Force (AUMF) bill put forward in response to the September 11 terrorist attack on America.

The daughter of an army officer, and the former wife of a member of the air force, she based her opposition to the AUMF bill on the 1964 Gulf of Tonkin Resolution that paved the way for expanded warfare in Vietnam. Hoping that we would have learned from our mistakes in Vietnam, she said: "We must be careful not to embark on an open-ended war with neither an exit strategy nor a focused target."

Congresswoman Lee introduced bills to repeal the AUMF year after year. Support for her repeal bill, mostly among Democrats, grew slowly and gradually. By 2017, however, the majority of members of the House Appropriations Committee, both Republican and Democratic, voted in favor of a repeal bill. The Speaker of the House, Paul Ryan, did not allow that bill to come to a vote.

In 2019, with the AUMF having been used to justify military force in more than 40 countries over 18 years, Lee's repeal bill was passed by the (Democratic-majority) House, as an amendment to the Defense Appropriations Act (DAA).

The repeal provision was not part of the Republican-majority Senate's version of the DAA — the version that was ultimately passed. It is reasonable to anticipate that Lee will introduce her bill again in the next Congress.

Wounded Warriors: Caring for Our Vets

The Veterans Administration (VA) is charged with caring for our veterans after their years of service, including medical care. Located across the country, each major VA hospital has particular areas of expertise, in addition to broader care services. In Houston, Texas, their specialties are cardiac and lung surgery. In Palo Alto, California, specialties are polytraumatic brain and spinal injuries. The other poly-trauma centers are at VA hospitals in Richmond, Virginia, Tampa, Florida, and Minneapolis, Minnesota.

Bay Area Veterans Administration hospitals have also focused on the development of innovative programs to address and alleviate PTSD, drug use, and homelessness among veterans of the Vietnam War and recent conflicts in the Middle East and Asia.

Twenty-six VA facilities serve the 270,000 veterans who live in the six-county San Francisco Bay Area. Central within that is the VA's Palo Alto Health Care

System (PAHCS), one of the largest and most complex VA facilities in the nation. PAHCS provides services to approximately 130,000 veterans with three inpatient divisions.

Among its 3,200 members, the PAHCS staff includes 800 veterans committed to serving their brothers and sisters in the service; a total of 2,600 community volunteers provide added support for VA patients.

One all-out PAHCS campaign is focused on helping homeless vets build a new life, including finding a place to live and a job. Toward that end, the facility has opened small clinics throughout the region to reach out to veterans who are isolated and may be unaware of the help available.

Happily, there are many success stories of injured veterans from across the state and the country who came to the Bay Area for the support and services that they were not able to find at home.

Terry, Jack, and Jason

Specialist Terry K. scoots around a throng of patients, visitors, and staff in the wide hallways of the Veterans Administration hospital in Palo Alto, California, on the Peninsula, south of San Francisco. She trades quips with patients as she maneuvers expertly among the wheelchairs and gurneys on her way to her job in the rehabilitation unit. Slim and healthy, shoulder-length blond hair shining, she is vibrant and confident in her role as a healer for her comrades returning from battle in Iraq and Afghanistan. It's a real surprise when she says proudly, "I've been sober five years now."

Terry returned home to the city of Stockton, in California's Central Valley, from her tour of duty. Like many other returning vets, her severe post-traumatic stress disorder (PTSD) went undiagnosed and untreated. She quickly became homeless, addicted to drugs for more years than she cares to detail, and unable to find help. She felt alone and abandoned by the military and the people she had pledged to serve.

"It's been a very long road," Terry admits, her blue eyes filling with tears as she tells her story. "I was 19 years old and a specialist in Wiesbaden, Germany. On my way to my first post, a civilian raped me. When I got to my post, I told my commander about it. He said he was sorry but did nothing. That was it."

She spent the next three years in service, singled out as a young and vulnerable woman without protection from her superiors. Her fellow soldiers took advantage of the situation, as they knew no one was going to discipline them. Terry never knew when she might be attacked or harassed. With only three other women in her unit to talk to, there was no help or support for her at the time.

Terry found a small satellite VA clinic in Stockton to seek help for a medical problem. The staff saw a vet hooked on drugs, with serious PTSD problems and no place to live. They could help her immediate health problem, but they had no resources to give her long-term emotional support and practical assistance. The VA staff knew that if Terry were going to get the help she really needed, they would have to get her to the Bay Area. So, they bundled her up and drove her more than 80 miles to the VA's Homeless Veterans Rehabilitation Program (HVRP) in Menlo Park, part of the Palo Alto VA complex. This center treated Terry's medical issues and saved her life in a deeper, lasting way. The program helped her get off the drugs and the street, taught her work skills and independence, and helped her return to a productive life.

Today, Terry radiates skill and self-confidence. Her employee identification tags swing across her chest as she hurries to her next assignment, helping veterans like herself adjust to civilian life after returning from battle abroad. "I didn't know there was any help out there," she says, still emotional as she speaks about her former life. "I wasn't aware of the world around me. I'd probably be dead if I'd stayed in Stockton."

Terry K. credits her good fortune to the commitment of the Bay Area's military outreach programs for veterans, as does Jack. Like so many returning soldiers, Jack came home from his tour of duty in Iraq and struggled to adjust to civilian life. Like Terry, he suffered severe PTSD and eventually lost his apartment. He spent more than three years homeless, living on the streets, grabbing shelter where he could.

It was the Oakland VA that helped him get back on his feet through the Bay Area's Homeless Veterans Rehabilitation Program. Like Terry, Jack has his pride back once again.

Outreach from San Francisco Bay Area veterans' facilities helps these wounded warriors get their lives back. For many, it is difficult to remember they were once high-functioning members of the military making a difference to their unit and to their country. How could everything have gone so wrong? Whom could they turn to, and would they even want anyone to know they were in such bad shape? Unfortunately, this scenario is played out all over the country.

Fortunately, Jack and Terry were able to make a connection that made a dramatic difference for them and in the lives of many others like them.

These VA programs also help vets like Jason Poole, who came to the Palo Alto VA to get his life back.

As was widely reported in the media, Poole's life was shattered to the point that no one believed he would function on even a minimal scale ever again. A 23-year-old marine corporal, his body was torn apart by a roadside bomb in Iraq. At that moment, it was questionable whether he would live, and if he did, whether he would be able to function in the world. Poole has had to learn all over again two things most of us take for granted: how to walk and how to talk. For Jason, the effort to find words or concentrate on putting one foot in front of the other is a struggle.

Before the bomb, he was popular with the girls, loved to have fun, and was always quick with a joke. Somehow, deep inside, the old Jason Poole is still intact. His personality — funny, kind, and outgoing — hasn't been shattered, although most of the rest of him was.

Poole's unit was among the first to invade Iraq. He was on his third tour of duty there, a week from coming home and leaving the marines, when he was wounded. He was on a foot patrol near the Syrian border on June 30, 2004, when the bomb went off. Shrapnel tore into the left side of his face and flew out from under his right eye. The force of the blast fractured his skull in several places and injured his brain. Part of his jawbone was smashed, and every bone in his face, including his nose and part of his eye sockets, was broken.

A helicopter flew him to a military hospital in Iraq and then to Germany, where surgeons cut a plug of fat from his abdomen and mixed it with other materials to seal an opening in the floor of his skull. From there he was transferred to the National Naval Medical Center in Bethesda, Maryland. His family flew in from all over the world to be with him. A week later, he was transferred to Bethesda Naval Hospital, still in a coma. His parents were told he might never wake up.

"I was unconscious for two months," Poole says. "One month and 23 days, really."

When he did wake, his parents had him transferred to the VA Hospital in Palo Alto. He arrived unable to speak or walk, drooling, with the left side of his face caved in, his left eye blind and sunken, a feeding tube in his stomach, and an opening in his neck to help him breathe. Today Jason is blind in his left eye and deaf in his left ear. He suffers with weakness on his right side. His face was rebuilt with skin and bone grafts and nearly a hundred titanium screws and plates. Still, he is happy to be alive and considers himself lucky. A big hunk of that luck was the medical treatment he received in the Bay Area.

Walking the corridors of the hospital is humbling and disturbing. The halls are filled with veterans, both young — barely out of their teens — and old, veterans of Vietnam, Korea, and World War II.

The Palo Alto VA is part of group in the Bay Area that serves the region; these medical facilities, along with Stanford Medical Center and the University of California at San Francisco, coordinate their expertise and provide care as a team. This is why veterans like Corporal Poole and his family come to the Bay Area.

Returning from the heightened experience of the battlefield to ordinary activities like school, work, and the kids' Little League practice is hard enough for those vets who somehow escape unscathed; it is doubly difficult for those suffering with PTSD, like Terry and Jack, and for those recovering from serious physical injuries, like Jason. Lack of employment makes the transition even more difficult. Without a job, the sense of loss and purpose only magnifies the contrast between military and civilian life. Too many veterans come home and feel life has nothing for them or find too little help to make a difference.

For the families at home, understanding what the military spouse or child is experiencing is often distressing. "While the veteran is trained to handle difficult situations, families are not," explains Chuck Arnold, coordinator of the veteran's program at the University of Medicine and Dentistry of New Jersey. "There needs to be more education and training for families, to include children."

It is unfortunate, but VA services are not equal across the country, or even within California, as Terry discovered in Stockton, and as veteran Eli Painted Crow found in Merced County. Although he lives just 200 miles east of San Francisco, he can't get qualified physical therapy there. The availability of services is particularly bad in rural areas. With facilities lacking around the country, veterans are traveling to the Bay Area from as far away as Virginia to receive vital services, even temporarily.

One such veteran came from southwest Virginia, where many veterans have depression and PTSD, but there is no one is there to help them navigate the system. This veteran said, "I have PTSD. I tried counseling at the Salem [Virginia] VA; it was bad. My issues never got resolved. Sometimes I would go for counseling, and they would ask me why I was there! I'd never see the same person twice. Every time I'd go, there was a different counselor."

The demand is also overwhelming in Corpus Christi, Texas. Demand has grown to 50 to 75 phone calls a week by veterans requesting help, but office director Abel Chapa says that he has no resources to handle even a small fraction of the demand. At best, he can accommodate only one or two callers a day. Chapa doesn't accept appointments because his "office" is part of the courthouse that used to be a credit union; it doesn't have a waiting area, and the door is kept locked. When vets come for help, they have talk to a secretary through a bank teller's window.

Community Support

The challenge for the VA is to provide effective programs for rehabilitation, and then to find those vets who have fallen into the cracks of American society to link to these programs. The San Francisco Bay Area VA has launched an all-out campaign to find these homeless vets and bring them in to a residential VA facility in Menlo Park.

In 1994, Vance Vanier, a Stanford University student interested in medicine, began visiting the patients at the Palo Alto VA Medical Center's geriatric unit. Vanier felt great connection to and compassion for the vets.

"We live in an age where the elderly and veterans of our nation are increasingly ignored or forgotten," he explains. "As their memories fade, we lose their stories of past generations who have contributed to our welfare suffer from society's indifference."

Vanier talked with his friends about his experiences and inspired several dozen other Stanford students to join him in the visits. Over time, the group became United Students for Veterans Health (USVH), expanding to other VA hospital across the country. The USVH's national headquarters are located in the Haas Center for Public Service at Stanford University.

Kerri Childress served as the Communications Officer and Congressional Liaison of the Palo Alto VA Hospital and moved to the Bay Area from Washington, DC, for her job. She likes to tell the story about the support from the community in building a home for visiting family of patients in the Palo Alto VA hospital. Called Fisher House, named after real estate developer and philanthropist Zachary Fisher, the homes were created to accommodate the families of the veterans who lived more than 50 miles away from the VA hospital. The guests stay free of charge.

"When a family travels here to be with a loved one mangled from battle, the last thing they need to be worried about is how to pay for a hotel bill. Some travel thousands of miles from their homes to get to Palo Alto."

The community raised more than $1.5 million in less than one year. The Fisher organization matched the proceeds, and the facility was opened in April 2006.

More than 80 similar Fisher Houses are situated at other VA facilities across the country and in Europe, partnerships forged among the Fisher House Foundation, the VA, and the respective communities. American values include respecting and supporting our returned warriors.

There is clearly plenty of evidence to dispute the accusations that the Bay Area is "antimilitary," Childress affirms.

"We have a big task ahead of us. The San Francisco Bay Area is right on board with us, and we get what we need because of them. The people here care for its military," Childress concluded. "We are anti-war; we are not anti-veteran."

A Brief Tour of the Bay Area's Military History

It is not surprising to find that the Bay Area is a major center for veteran care. Kaiser Permanente, one of the nation's earliest HMOs and largest health care plans, grew out of a health care scheme for Kaiser Construction employees who were building WWII battleships in Richmond's naval shipyards, near Oakland.

Those shipyards, and many other military facilities in the Bay Area, have long been shut down. San Francisco was an important military town for America from the

Spanish-American war through most of the 20th century, supporting 16 military stations around the Bay Area, including the Alameda Naval Air Station, the Presidio Army Base, Treasure Island Naval Station, and Fort Funston (formerly, the Lake Merced Military Reservation).

As in other cities and towns around the country, there were close ties between the military personnel and the communities that housed them.

Fort Funston is now one of the country's premier hang-gliding sites, as well as a favorite spot for shutterbugs, hikers, and picnickers. Fleet Week, a tradition in which our US Navy, Marine Corps, and Coast Guard strut their stuff in major cities across the country, is widely attended each year in San Francisco. The Presidio, now a majestically beautiful park, is also home to some of George Lucas's film production companies and the Disney Family Museum. The USS *Midway* moved to San Diego. The USS *Hornet*, still in the Bay Area, is now a museum ship. The other military installations have all been decommissioned. What happened?

Beginning in the 1960s, two major factors figured into changes in San Francisco's relationship with the military. One was the result of national changes in military placements, which included a disproportionate shift of bases to the southeastern part of the United States. The second was due to activist opposition to certain political and military policies.

The federal government, seeking efficiency and cost controls, began to shut down military bases around the country — first, one by one, and then several at a time — throughout the 1970s and '80s. Nine of 16 military facilities in the Bay Area were closed during those years. Closures were pursued even more aggressively after the end of the Cold War in the 1990s, under the direction of the bipartisan Base Realignment and Closure Commission (BRAC).

War and Peace, and Love, in San Francisco

> Congress shall make no law...abridging the freedom of speech, or of the press; or the right of the people peaceably to assemble, and to petition the Government for a redress of grievances.
> — *First Amendment to the US Constitution*

San Francisco Bay Area support for the men and women in our military is long-standing. Fighting against putting those troops in harm's way — in a war that is seen as wrong-headed — is indeed but another aspect of that support.

American freedom to express opposition to government decisions, including taking sometimes politically unpopular positions, continues to be part of the collective mindset of the Bay Area, particularly since the mid-1960s.

How did we evolve to that situation?

The first half of the 20th century saw America go through the First World War, the Roaring Twenties, the Great Depression, and the Second World War.

Tom Brokaw referred to the soldiers of World War II as the "Greatest Generation." American troops went overseas, to Europe, North Africa, Asia, and the Pacific. Starting with an American army that was smaller than the army of Portugal, the country built a war machine, with air and sea capacities larger than any other in the world. Construction and manufacturing in support of the war effort finished pulling us out of the Depression, and the economy was solid and growing.

Brokaw's description was that our men and women had gone to battle and they successfully did what they had to. Then, when they came home, they didn't talk about what they'd done. Rather, they settled in to enjoy the peace that they had earned.

As reflected on *Happy Days*, a TV program that aired in the '70s, the 1950s was a time when the suburbs expanded, and a strong middle class flourished. The local bad-boy rebel, "the Fonz," actually rode a motorcycle and had success with the girls. Oh, my!

General Dwight D. Eisenhower, who had successfully commanded the Allied forces in Europe, was elected as our president in November 1952. The emerging US-Soviet Cold War, the Korean War (1950–53), and the excesses of Senator Joseph McCarthy in hunting Communists in government and industry were mostly subsumed under the economic growth and family-raising of the '50s. The children of that decade were referred to as the "Silent Generation." Even the school-based "duck and cover" drills, conducted so the kids could be prepared for a feared Russian nuclear attack, were taken in stride.

But problems within our society were beginning to bubble, at first under, and then breaking through, the surface. In particular, African American GIs who had fought for equality and justice in the world, came back to continuing racial discrimination at home. Jim Crow laws in the southern United States, a collection of state and local statutes that localized racial segregation, as well as uneven applications of the GI Bill, continued to segregate and relegate the black population to second-class citizenship, and that was not going to be accepted any longer.

The courts were one setting for emerging changes. In its 1954 decision in *Brown v. the Board of Education*, the Supreme Court ruled for an end to segregated schools, establishing the mantra that separate is not equal.

Communities were another setting. On her way home from work one day in December 1955, black seamstress Rosa Parks refused a bus driver's order to get up and give her seat to a white man. As she later explained it, her refusal wasn't because she was physically tired, but that she was tired of giving in. She was arrested. In response, a boycott by African Americans of the Montgomery bus system was initiated. The boycott lasted 381 days, ending with a Supreme Court ruling that declared segregation on public transit systems to be unconstitutional.

In 1957, Arkansas Governor Orval Faubus sought to block the enrollment of black students in an up-until-then all-white school by calling up his state's National Guard. President Eisenhower sent federal troops to allow those first nine students to begin their integrated education.

At the same time, in Southeast Asia, Communist Ho Chi Minh's North Vietnamese troops were battling to take over Ngo Dinh Diem's anti-Communist South Vietnam. President Eisenhower promised US support to the South Vietnamese.

Newly elected President John F. Kennedy sent a team to study the situation in Vietnam in 1961; they returned to advise a buildup of American military, economic, and technical aid in order to help Diem confront Ho Chi Minh's Viet Cong threat.

We went from 800 troops in Vietnam in the 1950s to 9,000 under Kennedy, to 500,000 troops fighting there under President Lyndon B. Johnson and General William Westmoreland in 1966. By that time, the war effort was being met with significant protests across the nation.

By the mid-1960s, America was riven by wide-ranging violence and social upheaval. In 1967, a total of 159 riots protesting racial discrimination and injustice roiled cities across the nation, ranging from Newark to Detroit to Davenport.

Leaders were assassinated, including Medgar Evans and President John F. Kennedy (1963), Martin Luther King (1968), Malcolm X (1965), and Robert Kennedy (1968).

Attempts to end racial discrimination included court actions, sit-ins on public transportation and at restaurant counters, and drives to register black voters. Many of these efforts were met with violence and murder.

San Francisco's emerging hippie community in the '60s drew young Americans from around the country. Many were seeking a counterculture that would allow them to drop out of normal society; others gradually became part of the protest movements.

Student activism erupted around the country along with the unrest with the civil rights movement. The free speech movement (FSM) began at the University of California at Berkeley in the fall of 1964, sparked by attempts to limit political activists on campus. It was founded by students who had participated in Mississippi's "Freedom Summer" and was fueled by the arrival of the first wave of baby boomers seeking to impact and improve conditions, to bring about change through organization. Police, who had been fairly well schooled on how to handle student demonstrations over the previous several years, ignored those lessons on December 2, launching instead violent assaults on the students at Berkeley's Sproul Hall, which only served to strengthen the movement.

One meme that emerged from those engagements was "Don't Trust Anyone Over 30."

By the beginning of 1965, the anti-war movement base, distressed with escalating numbers of American troops who had served in Vietnam, had coalesced on campuses.

Our participation in the war in Vietnam, seen by many as unnecessary, unfair, and illegal, with increasing number of troops and casualties, built on a widely resented draft system, was a fulcrum of anti-war resistance across the country. The first large-scale protests against the war were mounted in 1964. In 1967, the world saw anti-war marches at the United Nations and at the Pentagon. These activities culminated in the Vietnam

Moratorium, massive demonstrations and teach-ins on October 15, 1969, followed by a Moratorium March on Washington, with more than half a million participants, one month later. Parallel demonstrations against the war took place in many other cities.

San Francisco in the 1960s

In San Francisco, school boards refused permission for high school students to take part in the second moratorium, declaring it "unpatriotic." Nevertheless, more than 50% of San Francisco high school students cut classes on November 15 as they went out to march against the war.

Protests against the Vietnam War were strong enough to persuade President Lyndon Johnson to announce that he would not run for re-election in 1968.

The war effort, which continued to increase under President Richard Nixon following his election in 1968, was particularly notable for bombings in urban areas and military incursions into Cambodia.

Some of the anti-war efforts focused on the troops returning home from Vietnam. In contrast to the heroes' welcomes that greeted troops returning from World War II, both anti-war activists and some older veterans met returning Viet vets with hostility, including, because of the bombings of civilians, shouts of "Baby killers!"

The beatnik movement in San Francisco, which coalesced around the beat poets of the 1950s, began to morph into San Francisco's emerging hippie community in the '60s. Dr. Timothy Leary, fueled in part by the psychedelic drug LSD, provided the mantra for the group: "Turn on, tune in, drop out."

Young Americans were drawn to the movement from around the country. Many joined the hippie counter-culture that allowed them to drop out of normal soci-ety. Some chose, instead, to gradually become part of the anti-war protest movements, which culminated on November 15, 1969, in Golden Gate Park, when 350,000 people from all walks of life and widely varying political persuasions marched, rallied, and staged the biggest anti-war demonstration ever seen in the West.

A number of the earliest San Francisco hippies were former students at San Francisco State University, who became intrigued by the developing psychedelic hippie music scene. These students joined the bands they loved, living communally in the large, inexpensive Victorian apartments in the Haight-Ashbury area.

By June 1966, some 15,000 hippies had invaded the Haight. Singing groups, including The Charlatans, Jefferson Airplane, Big Brother and the Holding Company, and the Grateful Dead, all moved to the Haight during this period.

The Diggers became the center of much of the activ-ity in the community. They combined spontaneous guer-rilla street theater, anarchistic action, and art happenings in their agenda to create a "free city." By late 1966, the Diggers opened free stores that simply gave away food, distributed free drugs, gave away money, organized free music concerts, and performed works of political art.

As a result of the massive and much-publicized November 15, 1969, anti-war activities, young people wanting to be part of the action began to flood into the Bay Area from all over the world. Tourists also came to see the "Peaceniks" lounging and strolling along the streets of San Francisco and Berkeley. The hippie community was known, at least in part, for communal living, drugs, and a good amount of casual sexuality, perhaps most clearly limned during the 1967 Summer of Love.

Typical of the flower children was Sunflower Evans, formally known as Janice Evans. She stood at the corner of Haight and Ashbury Streets each day, flashing the two-finger peace sign to passing motorists, her bell-bottom jeans festooned with cross-stitched flowers, her long hair falling around her shoulders.

"San Francisco (Be Sure to Wear Flowers in Your Hair)" was a hallmark song of the era. It reached fourth place on the American music charts in 1967 and was the number one song in Europe and the United Kingdom.

A Vietnam Veteran Comes Home

Vietnam veteran Michael Blecker returned stateside in 1970 after serving with the 101st Airborne. He anticipated going home to Reading, Pennsylvania, to start living his "real life." He didn't plan to become an activist.

But, as with so many returning veterans, things didn't fall into place so easily. He no longer felt at home in Reading. Eventually, he headed west to Northern California, joining a group of Vietnam veterans who had been assigned by VISTA (Volunteers in Service to America) to work in Bay Area Veterans Administration facilities.

He was troubled by what he found: traditional veterans' service groups like the American Legion and the Veterans of Foreign Wars (VFW), populated by World War II and Korean War veterans, were treating Vietnam veterans as defeated warriors, calling them malcontents, junkies, and crybabies. He realized that Vietnam vets would have to take care of their own in the peace, just as the "grunts had saved each other's asses in the war."

Blecker attended UC Berkeley, where he discovered a like-minded group of anti-war veterans. He joined the Vietnam Veterans Against the War (VVAW). Today, he is as proud of his service with the VVAW as he is of his service in the 101st Airborne.

Through the VVAW, Blecker met Bay Area lawyers who were doing draft counseling with active duty GIs, and these experiences encouraged him to go to law school.

In 1974, having made San Francisco his new hometown, Blecker drew upon resources from VISTA and VVAW as the building blocks for Swords to Plowshares, a service organization devoted to helping military veterans with basics ranging from a place to sleep all the way to legal representation when needed. Swords to Plowshares was founded in 1974 by six veterans who had been assigned as VISTA volunteers to work in Bay Area Veterans Administration (VA) facilities. They became particularly concerned that the VA was not properly addressing the unique needs of returning Vietnam veterans who had used or been exposed to Agent Orange.

Swords to Plowshares was the first Vietnam vet support organization in the United States. It was certified by the Veterans Administration, and it secured a federal grant to focus on the Agent Orange problem for agencies representing veterans who suffered health disorders as a consequence of Agent Orange exposure, including those suffering from PTSD. Their program served as a model for others around the country.

In more recent years, Blecker's organization has provided support to other Bay Area services for veterans, including Veterans Connect, which scours the neighborhoods for down-and-out vets who are homeless or disconnected from society in one way or another.

San Francisco values are not simplistically anti-war. While "Give Peace a Chance" is one favorite Bay Area bumper sticker, there was at least mixed support in 1991 for Operation Desert Storm, the six-week war launched under President George H. W. Bush in response to Iraq's invasion of Kuwait. The president made his case to the United Nations, gaining support of the Security Council, including the Soviet Union, directing Iraq to withdraw.

When Iraq did not bring their troops back home, a multi-national military force, led by the United States and including other NATO, Egyptian, and several other Arab nations' troops, did force Iraq's withdrawal, after which military actions ceased.

The Bay Area response was in sync with the national response in 2001. Five days after the 9/11 attacks, in which Al Qaeda suicide bombers hijacked four airliners and used them to attack the Eastern seaboard of the United States, destroying New York's World Trade Center twin towers and part of the Pentagon in Washington DC, the San Jose *Mercury News* reported on a reader poll that found the following:

> An overwhelming majority of Bay Area residents — almost nine in 10 — back military action against the terrorists who demolished the World Trade Center, ripped into the Pentagon, and fractured the nation's sense of security in Tuesday's violent strikes. About seven in 10 are willing to commit U.S. troops to combat — even if there is a substantial risk of American casualties.

Sadly, a war was launched in 2003 by President George W. Bush and Vice President Dick Cheney, with the support of but a few coerced allies, drawing upon inaccurate and misused intelligence. The military activities were seen as misfocused and mismanaged, and they were initiated without any vision of how to conclude the project. That war continues 17 years later.

Support for this military action dissipated rapidly, in the Bay Area as elsewhere.

The Bay Area's activist values are not all concentrated on one side of the political spectrum. In 2007 and 2008, for example, both anti-war activists and pro-military demonstrators faced off regarding attempts to shut down a marine recruitment center in Berkeley's downtown area. The Berkeley City Council approved and issued a letter on February 13, 2008, communicating support for the troops but opposition to the war.

Gays in the Military

The irony of the 1993 legislation known as Don't Ask, Don't Tell (DADT) was not lost on the many lesbians and gays who served, and continue to serve, honorably in our nation's military.

Officially, the military did not exclude or discharge homosexuals from its ranks, although sodomy (usually defined as anal and sometimes oral sex between men) was considered a criminal offense as early as Revolutionary War times.

DADT was legislation that was rooted in the attempt to remove bans on homosexuals in military service. It ended up as a failed compromise — theoretically, allowing gays to serve so long as they didn't admit it. Some 14,000 men and women were discharged from service for homosexuality in the ensuing 17 years.

Zoe Dunning of San Francisco, a retired navy commander, waited and advocated for change in the system for 17 years. She came out as a lesbian in 1993, and was one of the first people to challenge DADT. She won, but her case was deemed "unacceptable by military leaders" — meaning she remained in the service, but others were unable to use the same defense. She retired in 2007, perhaps the only openly gay person serving in the US military during those years. She joined the board of the Service Members Legal Defense Network (SLDN) in 1993, and became board co-chair in October 2006. SLDN, a national nonprofit, offered legal services to military personnel affected by Don't Ask, Don't Tell.

Commander Steve Clark Hall's story is more typical of those who flew, walked, and sailed under the radar.

Before his retirement, Hall served in the navy for 20 years, as commanding officer of the nuclear submarines USS *Greenling* and USS *Drum*. Hall says he is typical of the gays in the military. His service, he says, was not better — or worse — than any other soldier, sailor, or grunt, gay or straight. He is very proud of his years in the navy.

Discrimination exists in many organizations, but the military institutionalized it far longer than most. Although it seems reasonable to many that people asked to serve their country and make "the ultimate sacrifice" should have at least some equality within their unit, such had not been case for hundreds of years.

Lieutenant Colonel Victor J. Fehrenbach followed the example of his parents. His father was an air force lieutenant colonel; his mother was an air force nurse and captain. In the 18 years he served his country as an F-15E pilot, also known as a fighter weapons systems officer, Lieutenant Colonel Fehrenbach received nine air medals. On September 11, Fehrenbach was picked to be part of the initial alert crew immediately after the 9/11 attacks. A war hero, Fehrenbach flew numerous missions against Taliban and al-Qaeda targets, including the longest combat mission in his squadron's history.

With only two years left until his retirement, Lieutenant Colonel Fehrenbach was thrown out of the air force in 2009 because of he was outed by a third party as being gay. Being discharged after 18 years of service to his country meant he lost his retirement pension of $46,000 per year and all his military benefits, including health insurance. There was public outcry from the gay community as well as civil liberties organizations.

Fehrenbach fought the discharge, and he was allowed to finish his last two years to retirement at a desk job.

In reporting on his story, Rachel Maddow observed: "Just once, I wanted to hear someone explain why the United States is stronger, safer, and more secure with Lieutenant Colonel Fehrenbach out of the military."

As senator and former US Army lieutenant colonel and helicopter pilot Tammy Duckworth pointed out:

> When I was bleeding to death in my Black Hawk helicopter after I was shot down, I didn't care if the American troops risking their lives to help save me were gay, straight, transgender, black, white or brown. All that mattered was they didn't leave me behind.

The history and cost to the military in supporting a discriminatory policy, as well as to the individuals involved, has been great. As the United States prepared for World War II, psychiatric screening became a part of the induction process, and psychiatry's view of homosexuality as an indicator of psychopathology was introduced into the military. The military changed its policies so as to eliminate homosexual persons, based on a medical profile. In 1942, the revised army mobilization regulations included a paragraph that defined people as either homosexuals or normal and clarified procedures for rejecting gay draftees. Those who wanted to avoid getting drafted would devise some sort of act or action to insinuate that they were homosexuals. In one case, legend has it, a draftee showed up, saying nothing, but with polished toenails.

The military had conflicting standards when it came to filling the ranks. For example, homosexuals were allowed to serve only when there were personnel shortages. Screening procedures were relaxed, and many homosexual men and women enlisted and served. It wasn't clear how examiners determined who was gay and who was not.

Nevertheless, the shift was temporary. As the need for recruits diminished near the end of World War II, anti-homosexual policies were enforced with increasing vigilance, and many gay men and lesbians were involuntarily discharged. Throughout the 1950s and 1960s, acknowledging a homosexual orientation barred an individual from military service.

A new movement emerged in the United States in the 1970s that pressed for civil rights for gay men and lesbians. The military policy was one target of this movement.

The Government Accounting Office (GAO) reported that nearly 17,000 men and women were discharged under the category of "homosexuality" in the 1980s. The navy was disproportionately represented, accounting for 51% of the discharges even though it comprised only 27% of the active force during this period. White women represented 6.4% of personnel but 20.2% of those discharged for homosexuality.

By the end of the 1980s, reversing the military's policy was emerging as a priority for advocates of gay and lesbian civil rights. Several lesbian and gay male members of the armed services came out publicly and vigorously challenged their discharges through the legal system.

In 1992, legislation to overturn the ban was introduced in Congress. By that time, grassroots civilian opposition to the Department of Defense's policy of discrimination appeared to be increasing. Many national organizations had officially condemned the policy, and many colleges and universities had banned military recruiters and Reserve Officers' Training Corps (ROTC) programs from their campuses in protest of the policy.

The Servicemembers Legal Defense Network, quoting the Government Accounting Office, noted that it has cost more than $200 million to replace service members fired under Don't Ask, Don't Tell.

They also reported that the United States is home to more than one million gay veterans, most of whom served under the radar.

In the middle of his 1992 presidential campaign, candidate Bill Clinton pledged to follow the model of Harry Truman's historic executive order in 1948 ending racial segregation in the armed services with an end the ban on gays in the military.

After his election, Clinton tried to move forward to fulfill that pledge, but he ran into a sizable military and congressional group expressing fears that having openly gay troops would hurt morale and cause problems in the ranks. General Colin Powell, chairman of the Joint Chiefs of Staff; Senator Sam Nunn, chair of the Senate's Armed Services Committee; and President Clinton struck the compromise, which ended up as

Don't Ask, Don't Tell. Homosexuals in service were effectively moved from banned to silenced.

A National Decision

Seventeen years later, on December 22, 2010, President Barack Obama signed a new law that repealed Don't Ask, Don't Tell. For the first time in history, members of the gay, lesbian, and bisexual communities were allowed to serve openly in America's military.

Rather than coming directly at a congressional repeal, Obama first asked his Joint Chiefs of Staff to study the issues that might emerge if DADT was repealed, and also to study how to implement such a repeal if passed.

Their strong support for repeal — all branches except the marines supported it — helped get the legislation through the Senate with enough votes to prevent a conservative Republican filibuster; final passage was by a vote of 65 — 31. A transition year was built into the legislation, allowing time to set policies, procedures, and training in place.

While legislation doesn't immediately change individual prejudices, the repeal of DADT supports legal equality.

It was believed that the repeal of Don't Ask Don't Tell in 2010 finally removed LGBTQ service restrictions; the current administration in Washington, however, has once again been raising some barriers.

With the repeal of DADT, it can be suggested that the rest of the country finally has caught up with San Francisco.

As a strong anti-war region, the Bay Area demonstrates that it does not turn its back on those who fight for our freedom. Ideals and attitudes in favor of peace, combined with strong caring and support, inform the area's approach to our active troops and our veterans. From Barbara Lee's foresight in questioning Congress's giving open-ended war powers to the president to the repeal of Don't Ask, Don't Tell, the majority of Americans have now enlisted in supporting San Francisco values.

Take Action

1. **War powers.** When it comes to war, peace, and our national security, take a good look at the reasons that those in or seeking leadership positions offer when they want to take America to war. Elect those who truly have the defense of the country as their goals, rather than the position of their party or their big donor corporations.

2. **The VA.** The Department of Veterans Affairs has had several widely publicized failures to adequately serve their clients. In particular, there is a lack of sufficient staff to serve those veterans who suffer from PTSD. Ask your representatives what they are doing to address and correct the problem, and vote for those who will.

3. **Homeless vets.** Be proactive. Encourage any homeless veteran you encounter to go to the nearest VA Medical Center, or call the National Call Center for Homeless Veterans at 877-424-3838.

4. **Be vocal.** Be sure that your representative knows your position on issues such as how we use our military and how we support our veterans.

CHAPTER 6

San Francisco Cares about Health Care and Personal Choice

Though the doctors treated him, let his blood, and gave him medications to drink, he nevertheless recovered.

— *Leo Tolstoy*

It was [Santa Clara County Public Health Officer Dr. Sara] Cody who would eventually lead her Bay Area cohorts to pull the trigger March 16 [2020] on the historic seven-county legal order — the first of its kind in the country — that required residents to "shelter-in-place," days ahead of Gov. Gavin Newsom's similar mandate for the entire state.

— *The Mercury News, on the Bay Area's coronavirus lockdown*

Health care is both a personal and a national concern. As with many other issues, the role of government can be seen as regulatory or prescriptive.

The regulatory role means that the government makes laws and regulations designed to protects our citizens against unsafe products or practices, and against price gouging or other predatory business arrangements.

Seventy-nine percent of respondents surveyed about drug costs said that US drug prices are unreasonable. And 63% said there's not as much regulation as there should be to help limit the price of prescription drugs.

The prescriptive role is when the government seeks to make rules that tell us what we can and can't do with our own bodies. America divides in multiple ways on this issue, as will be detailed below.

Pricing for Medical Care

We are told by the drug companies that they need to be free to set their own prices, so that they will have the incentives to do the research and testing needed to develop new drugs to fight infection and disease.

On the other hand, we see the outrage at drug companies that egregiously increase the prices on long-established medications, forcing many to choose between buying food or needed medicines.

Humalog, an Eli Lilly brand of insulin that was sold for $21 per bottle in the United States in 1996, was priced at $255 in 2016, which represents a 700% markup after adjusting for inflation. Just under 10% of American adults are now living with diabetes or prediabetes.

The price of a two-pack of EpiPens in 2014 was under $400; in 2016, it was over $700. These prices particularly impact the parents of children who can have severe allergic reactions to insect stings or particular foods.

The BBC reported that after Turing Pharmaceuticals acquired the rights to Daraprim, which treats toxoplasmosis, a parasitic affliction that affects people with compromised immune systems, the price in the United States increased from $13.50 a dose to $750 a dose; in the UK, the cost of a Daraprim pill was sixty-six cents.

To illustrate high US medications pricing, in July 2019 Senator Bernie Sanders took a dozen people with diabetes on bus from Detroit to Windsor, Canada, to buy insulin at a local pharmacy. By buying insulin in Canada, everyone had saved a lot of money. A vial that one woman said could set her back $340 in the United States had cost her about a tenth of that.

On top of that, there are increases in hospital charges for medications, including markups of 700% or more at nearly one in five hospitals, according to an analysis by the Moran Company. This means that if a hospital purchased a medicine for $150, the markup could result in patients being billed $1,050.

American values and San Francisco values are in sync with respect to the desire for governmental involvement in controlling drug prices.

Regulations

The American Hospital Association feels that there are too many governmental regulations on health care, and they lobby hard to reduce those regulations. Citizens recognize that it is those same federal regulations that provide some assurances on quality control, and they also mandate consumer support and protection by requiring both electronic medical record keeping and the privacy of medical records.

Standards for quality of care, both by physicians and in nursing homes, are generally state rather than national issues.

San Franciscans value and respect each person's right over their own body, believing that the government should not be making group medical decisions for us.

Let's take a closer look at five major medically related topics: unwanted pregnancies, sex education, women's health services, end-of-life decisions, and marijuana.

Unwanted Pregnancies

Americans did not respond well to China's one-child policy, which was in place from the late 1970s until 2015. The chairman of the US Congressional Human Rights Committee in 2015, Republican congressman Chris Smith, chaired some 29 Human Rights hearings about China's one-child policy. He called it "the most egregious systematic attack on mothers ever." He supported Democratic president Bill Clinton's linking of the policy to human rights concerns in considering our trade policies with China. Unwanted pregnancies were particularly an issue in China at that time, as it has been and continued to be around the world.

An unwanted and unplanned pregnancy poses three choices to the woman: abortion, adoption, or parenting.

Possible scenarios abound. The woman might be a teenager who believed she couldn't get pregnant the first time she had intercourse, or she might be an older mother with other children to care for and financial struggles. The pregnancy could be the result of a rape or incest, or simply the failure of a condom or other birth control method. The pregnancy could be set in a relationship with dangerous control and power issues that critically endanger the mother's well-being in some way. There could be any number of other personal circumstances.

In every case, a decision, rarely taken as casual, needs to be made. America divides on this issue.

There are religions that prohibit abortion. San Francisco values fully recognize the right of practitioners of such religions to eschew abortions — for themselves.

On the other hand, those religions are not seen as having the right to impose their tenets on others who don't practice that faith. Instead, the choice among abortion, adoption, and parenting is seen as an individual decision, to be made by the woman, in consultation with her physician for medical information. A truly caring and loving partner might be consulted. And the decision is rarely made lightly.

The plethora of literature about abortion ranges across the legal landscape from the religious to the deeply emotional. Some of it touches on behavior noted earlier as not fitting San Francisco values — situations in which people espouse their values and try to impose those values on others.

Then, there are the people who not only tell others what to do, but who often act in ways diametrically opposite to their claimed values.

"My situation is different" is the mantra that often accompanies that behavior...which is also labeled as hypocrisy.

An article by feminist and abortion rights activist Joyce Arthur shared a number of reports of such behavior. Here are two examples, the first from a physician, the second from a volunteer escort at a clinic:

> I have done several abortions on women who have regularly picketed my clinics, including a 16-year-old schoolgirl who came back to picket the day after her abortion, about three years ago...with the usual anti posters and chants. It appears that she got the abortion she needed and still displayed the appropriate anti views expected of her by her parents, teachers, and peers.

> In the Boston area, Operation Rescue and other groups were regularly blockading the clinics, and many of us went every Saturday morning for months to help women and staff get in. As a result, we knew many of the 'antis' by face. One morning, a woman who had been a regular 'sidewalk counselor' went into the clinic with a young woman who looked like she was 16-17, and obviously her daughter. When the mother

came out about an hour later, I had to go
up and ask her if her daughter's situation
had caused her to change her mind. "I don't
expect you to understand my daughter's
situation!" she angrily replied. The following Saturday, she was back, pleading with
women entering the clinic not to 'murder
their babies.'

Sex Education

People should have the necessary knowledge to
make informed decisions about their own health.

Legislation that prevents the sharing of scientifically-
based information, or, worse, that requires teaching false
information, does not serve our people well.

One approach that successfully reduces abortions is
the reduction of unwanted pregnancies, and young men
and women who are educated about safe sex have fewer
teen pregnancies.

A Pew Research study was conducted in states where
abstinence is mandated as at least part of sex education
courses. It is not uncommon for students in those states
to be asked to take "purity" or virginity pledges as part of
their curriculum. In one study, among girls who were in
grades seven and eight when the study began and who
had not yet had intercourse at that time, pledge takers
were found to be significantly more likely than non-
takers to become pregnant outside of marriage within
six years of their first sexual intercourse — 30% vs. 18%,

respectively. In both groups, 75-80% of these pregnancies were unplanned.

Those who had taken virginity pledges were also more likely to have tested positive for HPV than those who hadn't taken such pledges.

The authors of the research hypothesize that those "who took virginity pledges were less prepared when it came to practicing safe sex, perhaps because abstinence-only sex education courses have a tendency to downplay the effectiveness of condoms and contraceptives."

In 2009, Colorado began offering teens free IUDs without requiring parental consent. The *Denver Post* reported that, within eight years, teen pregnancies dropped 54%. Teen abortion rates fell by 64%. And, for every dollar spent on the program, the state saved $5.85 in labor and delivery costs, childcare assistance, and food stamps.

A 2017 infographic looked at sex education across the country. Twenty-four states mandate sex education. Eighteen states mandate the inclusion of information on contraception whenever sex education is taught; thirty-seven states mandate that information on abstinence be included, and twenty-six mandate that abstinence be stressed. Only thirteen states require that medical information in sex education courses be accurate. Thirteen states mandate that sexual orientation be included in the discussions; four states require that only negative information about sexual orientation be included.

Students in the San Francisco Unified School District (SFUSD) get a thorough education about health, including sex education. Students also have the opportunity to have a confidential session with a counselor. The lessons are appropriate for each age and grade level. It includes outreach, substance abuse, and LGBTQ support services. For a period of time, this education was "opt in," that is, parents could opt in to having their children enroll in the program.

California has implemented its Healthy Youth Act, mandating comprehensive sex education for students in grades seven to twelve. This decision fits in with San Francisco values that include wanting people to be able to make decisions about their own lives, and enabling them to do so effectively by providing valid information upon which those decisions can be made. This legislation does allow parents who don't want their kids to learn about issues like body image, contraception, and HIV awareness and prevention to formally opt out by submitting a document to their school or district.

The SFUSD mandates that the educations delivered be age appropriate, and that students receive comprehensive education, which includes health education that is factual, skills based, medically accurate, and objective. According to program directors, "all policies are reviewed, adopted, implemented, and updated to reflect current needs and to support all members of the school community, including teachers, staff and students."

Similarly, in 50 schools across Los Angeles County, students will be able to go to new Health and Wellness Centers to talk about depression, anxiety, stress management, substance abuse, reproductive health, and related issues. An individual's sexuality is treated as

one aspect of human health. The centers, a partnership uniting the efforts of the school district, Planned
Parenthood, and the LA County departments of public
health and mental health, will allow students to pop
in for help between classes, without needing to leave
school. Having access to tests for STIs or pregnancy right
on campus is seen as a potential game changer in the
health care of the students. The centers will not provide
abortions.

Since 1972, San Francisco Bay Area residents of all
ages have been able to benefit from the free, confidential, accurate, non-judgmental information about sex
offered on a telephone switchboard by SFSI, the San
Francisco Sex Information service.

The program, founded by a volunteer group of
nurses, has now divided itself into two separate groups:
SFSI itself continues to offer training for sex educators,
while the switchboard functionality of SFSI was spun off
into a new nonprofit organization: The SGR (pronounced
"sugar") Hotline.

. The availability of safe abortion and sex education are topics over which our country's divide into red
and blue states are dramatic. And so are the data on
outcomes.

The National Campaign to Prevent Teen
Pregnancy data shows that teenagers in Mississippi, the
reddest of red states, are more sexually active than the
teens of any other state; the teenagers of liberal New
York are the least active. Similar data can be found for
teen pregnancy, with nine of the ten worst states for
teen pregnancy rates being red states. If the red states

truly want to reduce teen pregnancies, — and, as a result, to reduce the number of abortions — they might do well to consider the California approach to effective sex education.

Researchers also found that having LGBTQ-inclusive sex education was associated with less adverse mental health among all students. Suicide is the second leading cause of death among the 10-to-24-year-old population who identify on the LGBTQ spectrum. Findings were that for every 10% increase in LGBTQ-inclusive sex education, there was a 20% reduction in reported suicide plans. In addition, there was significantly less bullying of gay/lesbian youth on school property.

Roe v. Wade under Attack

Family and personal values are major tinder points in the country. These issues include expressions of gender, same-sex marriage, reproductive rights and choices, and the many definitions of family.

One hallmark of the San Francisco Bay Area is an abiding respect for individual rights and individual choices, for the right to live and express one's own lifestyle, whatever that might be, without fear of the judgment or constraints of others, and resisting having those choices forced on others.

Multiple anti-abortion bills have recently been passed in conservative-controlled state legislatures. In 2019 alone, 16 states have filed, moved, or enacted six-week abortion bans. Nine states have passed bills that outlaw abortion or forbid it past a certain point in pregnancy. Louisiana, for example, outlaws all abortions after a so-called "fetal heartbeat" can be detected — long before most women even realize they're pregnant.

It has been observed that most of these laws are passed by male-dominated, Republican-dominated state legislatures — the same elected representatives who say they "want the government off the backs" of their citizens, but feel it is right and appropriate to have government involved in making medical decisions about the reproductive systems of the women among their constituents.

These laws also have a direct impact on other health issues for women. By restricting funding for agencies that offer information on abortion options, or that perform abortions, they are forcing the closing of many agencies across the country that are the only available general health services for women. Planned Parenthood is one major provider of such health care services.

This legislation is seen as setting the stage for a challenge to *Roe v. Wade*, the landmark Supreme Court decision that protects the fundamental "right to privacy" of pregnant women, which includes the liberty to choose whether or not to have an abortion. Conservatives believe the chances of overturning the fifty-year-old court decision are high, due to the Supreme Court's new conservative majority.

Some of this legislation includes legal penalties for physicians who operate to save a mother's life in cases of naturally occurring abortions of non-viable fetuses.

Alabama legislation, for example, allows exceptions for medical emergencies, but not for pregnancies caused by rape or incest. An Alaska bill would make performing or attempting to perform one a felony. There would be no exceptions for the life of the pregnant mother or for rape or incest victims.

With the arrival of the coronavirus in the spring of 2020, Alabama, Iowa, Ohio, Oklahoma, and Texas all halted abortions as being "non-essential," and not time sensitive, but rather as procedures that could be post-poned, and an appeals court upheld this position.

An independent poll released in January 2019 found that two-thirds of Americans think abortion should be legal in "all" or "most" cases, and 73% are opposed to overturning *Roe v. Wade*.

Residents of the San Francisco Bay Area continue to value safe and available choices, as part of providing strong health care and pregnancy services.

Women's Rights and Women's Health Services

San Francisco's Department on the Status of Women began to conduct gender analyses as the first step to advancing sound public policy that meets the needs of women and girls. They created two task forces, leading to a report titled "Girls in San Francisco, Benchmarks for the Future." This report presents a first-of-its-kind analy-sis and review on the status of San Francisco girls on social, economic, educational, health, and criminal justice issues.

One group, which focused on girls in the criminal justice system, found that girls who came into the juve-nile justice system arrived for very different reasons and with very different needs from boys in the system.

The second group emerged from an ordinance that San Francisco adopted in 1998 to implement CEDAW, the United Nations 1979 Convention on the Elimination of All Forms of Discrimination against Women. San Francisco was the first municipality in the United States to do so. As of 2015, 189 countries had adopted the treaty, some with reservations relating primarily to some aspect of sovereignty. President Jimmy Carter signed the treaty in 1980 for the United States, but it still awaits Senate ratification. San Francisco moved forward to implement CEDAW's goals, which fit well with San Francisco values: working to end discrimination against women and girls in political, social, and public life, including in health care, education, sports, and domestic options.

The first San Francisco focus was looking at human rights and discrimination issues throughout the city.

Women's health services in San Francisco generally include the availability of contraceptive services, appropriately selected abortion procedures, pre- and post-abortion patient education, and follow-up patient education to hopefully avoid repeated unwanted pregnancies going forward.

Initial pregnancy-related visits to Planned Parenthood's San Francisco Health Center clinic are described as including the following:
- a pregnancy test
- a chance to speak with a trained staff person about all available choices: abortion, adoption, and parenting
- a conversation with the health care provider about health history

- lab tests/blood work
- a pelvic exam
- an ultrasound
- medications to make an abortion more comfortable if elected
- medication if one is Rh negative
- antibiotics or other medications
- birth control information
- a birth control method

At the End of Life: Dying with Dignity

The Hemlock Society was founded in 1980 in California by Derek Humphries. Humphries, who had helped his wife, who was dying painfully of breast cancer, end her life five years earlier, sought and built a platform from which to advocate for legalization of physician-assisted suicide. His book, *Final Exit*, in combination with the activities of Dr. Jack Kevorkian, brought the question of physician-assisted suicide to public attention.

A ballot measure in California in 1992 was proposed by the Hemlock Society, to allow aid in dying. The ballot measure was soundly defeated.

Over the following decades, however, the concept took root.

As with many other social changes, end-of-life options are being adopted only slowly; and, as with many other social changes, West and East Coast states have led the way.

Oregon passed the first Death with Dignity Act in 1997. Oregon was followed by Washington in 2008 and Montana in 2009. Vermont passed its Patient Choice and

Control at End of Life Act in 2013, and a court ruling in New Mexico allowed for a limited patient's right to die.

In 2014, a 29-year-old California woman with terminal brain cancer moved, very publicly, to Oregon in order to take advantage of their Death with Dignity Act. The press coverage of that woman's case was a major factor in California's successful passage of an End of Life Option Act in 2015.

As of 2019, Colorado, the District of Columbia, Hawaii, New Jersey, and Maine have also enabled death with dignity. Maine's 2019 legislation, which is typical of physician-assisted suicide laws, allows mentally competent adult patients with terminal diseases that "within reasonable medical judgment, produce death within 6 months" to request medication that would end their lives. Multiple requests, and waiting periods between, are required.

While considering whether to sign California's legislation, Governor Jerry Brown wrote, "I do not know what I would do if I were dying in prolonged and excruciating pain. I am certain, however, that it would be a comfort to be able to consider the options afforded by this bill."

A 2017 poll by Gallup displayed that a solid majority of Americans, with 73% in favor, support laws allowing patients to seek the assistance of a physician in ending their life. In 2018, at least 25 states were considering legislation to permit physician-assisted suicide.

Opposition to this option was initially lodged in the physician community's American Medical Association. That opposition has softened considerably. David Grube, an Oregon physician who retired in 2012, initially opposed aid-in-dying. His position shifted, he indicated, when he saw that no evidence emerged to show patients were being pressured into the process. Opposition can also be found rooted in groups that seek to apply their personal religious beliefs to the personal medical issues of other people.

Governor Brown's signing statement once again illustrated valuing the individual's right to make their own informed medical decisions, and the Gallup poll again illustrates that San Francisco values do, indeed, match the values of much of America.

One Toke over the Line?

Famously tracking back to San Francisco's 1967 Summer of Love, Bay Area residents have long valued the recreational and medical use of cannabis and view its use as a valid personal choice. California also favors correcting the artificial, erroneous, and invalid federal categorization of marijuana as a Schedule 1 drug.

But back before its legalization in California, little Jonathan Lustig, from Mountain View, California, was a very unsettled eight-year-old. He was diagnosed with depression, migraine headaches, and both attention deficit and bipolar disorders. He was prescribed massive doses of anti-depressants as well as Ritalin, a drug that can have calming effects on children.

With those illnesses and the heavy medications, elementary school was a blur for Lustig. In 1991, at the age of 13, he stopped taking his pills and flushed them down the toilet. That is when he began smoking marijuana (cannabis). He began to feel better. Not drugged, just clear-headed and less anxious. At first, he didn't associate his sense of well-being, his improved ability to concentrate in school, and diminished depression with the illegal drug — that was, until he went on vacation with his family, and the negative symptoms and headaches came back. He soon realized that marijuana smoothed out his agitated mood and relieved his headaches. In the 1990s, he simply did what lots of other kids did: he bought his pot illegally on the street.

Lustig's path paralleled the evolution of marijuana legislation. In 1996, he became able to get his marijuana legally by prescription, but there were still limitations on its availability. As an adult, he became an advocate for safe local access to cannabis. In 2005, he sought to open a now-legal dispensary in his hometown of Mountain View, but the city council voted it down by a narrow majority, at least partially influenced by the intimidation that some felt from the presence of agents from the Drug Enforcement Agency at the council meeting. In 2006, he started a nonprofit marijuana collective, with direct delivery to patients with medical prescriptions.

President Obama instructed federal prosecutors to ignore those using and selling marijuana in compliance with state laws. Yet in some areas, the feds put pressure on marijuana sales by seizing the assets of owners of property where sales were taking place. Under Attorney General Jeff Sessions' Department of Justice, in January 2018, all US attorneys were directed "to enforce the laws enacted by Congress and to follow well-established principles when pursuing prosecutions related to marijuana activities."

This policy was published in direct opposition to the will and position of the American population. Pew and CBS polls showed that the 31% of Americans who favored the legalization of marijuana in 2000 had more than doubled in 2018.

Recreational plus medical uses of marijuana have become legal in 11 states, Washington, DC, and Guam, as of July 2019. Twenty-two additional states have legalized the medical use of marijuana. As with other social movements, the states leading are mostly on the West and East coasts: Alaska, California, Colorado, Maine, Massachusetts, Michigan, Nevada Oregon, Vermont, and Washington. And several candidates for the Democratic nomination for president in the 2020 election endorsed legalizing marijuana at the federal level.

Marijuana use has roots as far back as 2737 BCE. It has been referenced in ancient Chinese medicine, and soon spread from China to India, North Africa, and Europe by AD 500. Historically reported medicinal uses included treating rheumatism, gout, and malaria. It was a staple commercial crop in the United States in the 1600s, and it was listed in the *United States Pharmacopeia* from 1850 until 1942, to be used to treat a wide variety of ailments, including labor pains, nausea, and rheumatism.

A highly inaccurate propaganda movie, *Reefer Madness*, initially titled *Tell Your Children* and financed by a church group, was produced in 1936 and circulated in the 1940s and '50s as part of the Federal Bureau of Narcotics' emerging thrust against marijuana use. In the

1950s and 1960s, marijuana use was linked to the beat generation and then the hippies, and it was portrayed in the media as part of laid-back California counterculture.

By the mid-1960s, pot was readily available to kids in schools across the country. It wasn't until 1970, after almost 5,000 years of use, that marijuana was designated by the federal government as a Schedule 1 drug. Along with heroin and ecstasy, it was grouped with drugs having the highest potential for abuse, with potentially severe psychological or physical dependence, and with no accepted medical use.

Draconian and very unevenly applied laws and penalties were enacted in the years that followed. Additionally, extreme federal restrictions were placed on medical research on marijuana, preventing controlled testing of its potential medical benefits. Of added concern is that, lacking testing opportunities, possible drug interactions between marijuana and other medications cannot be studied. Significant anecdotal evidence details multiple positive effects of cannabis that range from fending off nausea and blocking pain in people with cancer and AIDS to reducing battle-induced PTSD to assisting those with sleep dysfunctions. According to a report in *Forbes*, new research done outside the United States shows that cannabis derivatives may successfully relieve painful symptoms in such other diseases as multiple sclerosis, Crohn's disease, and other inflammatory conditions.

Justice

San Francisco is making history as the first US city committed to expunging more than 9,000 marijuana

convictions — more than half of them felony convictions — under a section of Proposition 64 that legalized
the recreational use of the drug in 2016. That part of the
proposition was developed to remediate the extreme
and imbalanced sentencing for marijuana offenses in the
past.

District Attorney George Gascón stressed that this
action will dismantle the roadblocks faced by people
who, in job applications or other instances, must disclose
felony convictions. "What we're talking about is offering
people an opportunity to get housing, to get education,
to get employment...Felony convictions often, even if
you're a parent...may preclude you from participating in
school activities with your kids," he said.

Noting that marijuana-related convictions disproportionately affect low-income residents and people of
color, Gascón said that his office will present the thousands of cases to a judge to finalize the expungements.

Illinois passed similar legislation in 2019, and other
states are studying the same question.

The new US Attorney General William Barr, appointed
in 2019, said that he would discontinue the crackdown on
marijuana pursued by predecessor Sessions; outcomes
are yet to be seen.

There wasn't much of a choice for the US Food and
Drug Administration (FDA) when, in the spring of 2018,
it was deciding whether or not to give final approval to
Epidiolex, a brand-new cannabis-based drug developed
by Greenwich Biosciences, a California-based company.
Over multiple randomized, placebo-controlled drug
trials, the drug had been administered to 516 people

who were suffering from two rare forms of epilepsy. The results spoke for themselves: cannabis had reduced the amount and severity of seizures the patients experienced.

The FDA approved Epidiolex. This was, of course, a boon for people who suffer from these disorders, but it also undercut the federal government's prohibition of pot, which the feds still maintain has a high potential for abuse and no accepted medical use. It's a big deal: by approving Epidiolex, the FDA told the world that the government's history of cannabis prohibition is simply not valid.

The modern American medical marijuana movement was in large part launched in San Francisco in the 1980s and '90s, when a series of different forces coalesced around pot. In the 1980s, the HIV/AIDS epidemic was advancing through the gay community at a frightening pace, while the US government and the medical community either looked the other way or grossly stigmatized the people with the virus.

Meanwhile, California was already on its way to becoming an international hotbed of cannabis, with hippies using the consistent sun in the remote northern part of the state to breed new and more potent forms of pot, many of which form the staple cultivars sold across the world today. In the center of these two forces sat San Francisco, an ultra-liberal city that had both a large gay community and a political history of giving the feds the middle finger.

Unsurprisingly, the city's gay community discovered that pot was hugely helpful in treating the symptoms of

HIV/AIDS. One witness to pot's medical value was Dennis Peron, a Vietnam veteran living in San Francisco who saw how pot helped his HIV-positive partner. Peron, a close friend of Harvey Milk, was as much a political organizer as a pothead, and he started the country's first public dispensary, the San Francisco Cannabis Buyers Club, which later played an instrumental role in California's 1996 legalization of medical marijuana.

One person who saw this play out was Mary Lynn Mathre, a registered nurse, who in 1997 published a detailed manifesto of pot's medical qualities and uses. Her book eventually made its way to Geoffrey Guy, a British doctor and scientist, who was inspired to explore pot's medical properties. He went on to start his own company, GW Pharmaceuticals, which acquired a license from the British government to grow and study pot.

Twenty years later, Guy submitted a CBD drug for approval to the FDA that went by the name of — you guessed it — Epidiolex. When the drug was approved by the FDA, the movement started by San Francisco's gay community more than 30 years earlier was complete.

The US government finally admitted that pot is medicine. San Franciscans knew it all along.

Take Action

1. **Medical costs.** The majority of Americans want governmental help in controlling medical costs. What are the positions of candidates on our ballots regarding such controls? Support candidates who seek to support us, everyday citizens. Don't support candidates whose votes and positions

mirror the lobbying positions of the drug and health care industries.

2. **Abortion.** Recognize that abortion is a personal decision, between the patient and her physician. Recognize as well that it is a valid life and medical choice for some people in some circumstances. If you oppose a woman's unconditional right to choose, at least recognize and allow for such legitimate procedures in cases of rape, incest, or when the health of the mother is in danger. Consider the situations where young women you love may need to make that necessary choice, and allow them to do so safely.

3. **Sex Education.** Advocate for and support real information-based sex education for your kids, and support those local and national candidates who feel the same way. Share your values with your children, and be sure they have accurate facts as well as personal beliefs upon which they can make decisions in those difficult teen years. Remember that you don't want those children to be pregnant, or to have sexually transmitted diseases, because of ignorance.

4. **Health care.** Support candidates who support the provision of good health care services for all, and particularly for women.

5. **End of life.** Consider the options you would like to have when you or a loved one is close to death, and support candidates who support the option of dying with dignity.

6. **Marijuana.** We know, anecdotally, that marijuana can help some medical issues. Don't you want to know if marijuana interacts badly with other prescription medications you may take for your blood pressure or kidneys? Do you want to know whether marijuana use substantially leads to harder drugs? Support candidates and legislation that allow for the use of marijuana, and for study on the facts about the medical benefits and the potential problems there may be in marijuana use.

7. **Pot-related justice.** Understand the justice and fairness of adjusting old, long-term, heavily and unevenly penalized marijuana convictions. This isn't being "soft on crime"; it is redressing wrongs done to members of our community. Support candidates who have that understanding.

CHAPTER 7

San Francisco Supports Diversity and Immigration Reform

In the Bay Area, we don't just accept diversity — we embrace it.
— *Congresswoman Anna Eshoo*

I disagreed with just about everything George W. Bush did as President. And then, the one time that we were in total sync — the time he supported a truly comprehensive immigration package — his party beat on him and he backed away from it just a few days later.
— *San Francisco Bay Area resident*

I don't care how tall the fence is as long as the doors are big enough.
— *Conservative activist Grover Norquist*

Immigration is at the heart of the Americas. Immigrants settled this country and made this country

great. To be single-mindedly anti-immigration is to sim-
ple-mindedly deny our American heritage.

As we examine the history and behaviors reflecting
some of the current American attitudes relating to immigration, ask yourself how very bad would it have to
be for you to decide to take your three-year-old child,
or your three children under the age of ten, and begin a
2,400-mile journey on foot, carrying a child much of the
way. You might be willing to do so because you are flee-
ing terrorism or gang conscription of pre-teen children,
or because you want an opportunity raise your family in
a place where you will have an opportunity work in order
to have a decent life. And recognize that you would be
making that trip knowing that you are seeking to settle in
a country not your own, with a language not your own,
and leaving your friends and relatives behind.

Migration to the Americas

The original inhabitants of the United States were
Asian.

From Peru's Norte Chicos to the Plains Indians to the
Alaskan Yuits, indigenous tribes came to the Western
hemisphere from the North Asian area that is now
Siberia. Their path was created as one result of the most
recent maximum glacial expansion, some 22,000 years
ago, which led to a lowering of sea levels, creating the
Beringia land bridge between Asia and what would become the Americas.

The next major wave of immigration tracks through
the 15th through 18th centuries, when Western
Europeans and Africans (mostly as slaves) reached

these shores. Colonies were established along the East Coast, drawing predominantly from the populations of Spain, Holland, England, Scotland, Ireland, France, and Germany. In 1800, 81% of Americans were themselves or were descended from Northern Europeans.

The first major wave of immigrants after American independence came between 1820 and 1890, primarily from those same countries, with Scandinavians, Austrians, Poles, and increased numbers of Irish added in.

It was in 1876 that the Statue of Liberty, built in France, was mounted on an American-built base in New York's harbor, in celebration both of the American centennial and of the long-term friendship and alliances of the two countries.

The Statue of Liberty was seen as a celebration of the freedom and opportunities available to people who immigrate to the United States. Emma Lazarus was selected to write the inscription on the base, an inscription which, as those on both sides of the political divide have suggested, expressed an aspirational rather than real view of America's uneven immigration policies:

> Give me your tired, your poor,
> your huddled masses yearning to breathe free,
> the wretched refuse of your teeming shore.
> Send these, the homeless, tempest-tossed to me,
> I lift my lamp beside the golden door!

A second wave of European immigrants arrived between the 1890s and the 1920s, mainly from Southern, Central, and Eastern Europe.

Chinese immigration to the United States became significant in the 1850s and 1860s. The so-called "coolie trade" (*coolie* coming from the Hindi word for *wages*) began in Asia the late 1840s as a response to the universal need for paid unskilled laborers, a labor market brought on by the worldwide movement to abolish slavery.

Some adventurous Chinese miners, and larger numbers of support laborers, arrived in California after the discovery of gold, and additional workers arrived to be part of the labor force building the transcontinental railways in the 1860s. Along with work opportunities in the United States, the 1850-64 Taiping Rebellion in China, which incurred a death toll estimated anywhere between 20 million and 100 million people, stimulated the emigration from China.

Immigration from Japan expanded during the last quarter of the 19th century, reaching Hawaii first, and then the mainland. Filipino immigration increased during these years as well. As before, the flow was primarily of people seeking work, in response to our need for unskilled labor.

Two additional waves of Asian migrations were seen in the 20th century. Vietnamese, Cambodians, and Hmong arrived in the 1960s and 1970s, mostly as refugees following the Vietnam War. And migrants began to arrive from India starting just before the turn of the 21st century, in this case looking to fill the unmet need for educated professionals to work in technology.

Just as in the gold rush and railroad construction eras, America depends on immigrant labor to fill 21st century jobs that some Americans don't wish to do, including intensive work in fruit and vegetable fields and in food processing plants. At the professional end of the labor market, there are more jobs here than qualified skilled and well-educated candidates to fill them.

Richard Florida's *Citylab* article reports that Americans who were born elsewhere account for a fifth of all STEM (science, technology, engineering, and math) workers with a bachelor's degree, 40% with a master's degree, and more than half (54.5%) with a Ph.D. What's more, immigrants are significantly involved in anywhere from a third to a half of major high-tech startup companies. More than 40% of recently founded Silicon Valley tech companies have at least one immigrant on their founding team.

In a 2016 study, the International Monetary Fund concluded: "Immigration significantly increases GDP per capita in advanced economies."

America has been, and continues to be, built on an international base. One out of every four people living in the United States today is either a first- or second-generation immigrant.

As on so many issues, American values and San Francisco values have generally been in sync. The Latin phrase "E pluribus unum," generally translated as "out of many, one," appears on the Great Seal of the United States and can be most commonly seen on the one-dollar bill. The phrase was the unofficial motto of the United States starting in 1776, when it was selected by the committee developing the national seal. Generations of school children have been taught that we proudly identify our country as a melting pot, a nation of immigrants that has built its strength on the contributions of many cultures.

In 1956, an act of Congress that was viewed by many as a political response to the Cold War and Russia's "godless Communism" determined that we would adopt an official motto: In God We Trust. "E pluribus unum" continues to be considered as the unofficial American motto.

In 2001, following the September 11 attacks, a famous public service announcement prepared by the Ad Council and Texas ad agency GSD&M featured a series of ethnically diverse people, each saying, "I am an American," followed by a black screen showing only the phrase "E pluribus unum" and its English translation.

The treatment of immigrants across the country has ranged widely over the years, however, including some painfully negative chapters.

Those of us who grew up with grandparents who migrated to this country watched a very familiar pattern repeat in family after family, be they Latino, Jewish, Asian, European, Arab, or North African. The grandparents tended to work hard, learn enough English to do the generally low-level jobs they could find, continued to primarily speak their original language at home, and emphasized education as the way up in this society to their children. Their children (perhaps your parents or your grandparents) went to school — at least through high school, sometimes beyond — became fluent in English, and would often bug their parents, repeatedly telling them to "speak English, Ma!" And their kids? We're 100% American; if anything, we're a bit sorry that our parents didn't retain more of their parents' culture and language to share with us as part of our history. And that pattern continues to repeat with newer generations.

Dave Campos, an attorney and former San Francisco supervisor, was born in Puerto Barrios, Guatemala. When he was 14, his parents took him and his two sisters, and they fled to the United States to escape the Guatemalan Civil War. They entered illegally. Campos spoke no English when he arrived. He learned the language quickly enough to handle American academics, and he graduated at the top of his class at Jefferson High School in South Central Los Angeles. The quality of his work was such that he was able to attend Stanford University, and then Harvard Law School, on scholarships that he earned. He applied for and received legal status through a job. He worked for several law firms, became a deputy city attorney in San Francisco, and then served as San Francisco supervisor for District 9 from 2008 to 2016. A typical American story.

Immigration Facts Dispute the Fears

Separating facts from fiction about how immigrants fit into our society is important, as we consider current issues relating to immigration into the United States.

A 2018 study from the Brookings Institute analyzed the impact of immigrants in the United States in detail. Among the report's most compelling findings are:

- Output in the economy is higher and grows faster with more immigrants. The total annual contribution of foreign-born workers is roughly $2 trillion, or about 10 percent of annual GDP; the contribution of unauthorized immigrants is estimated to be about 2.6% of GDP.
- About three-quarters of the country's foreign-born population are naturalized citizens or authorized residents.

The other 25% of our immigrants are here illegally. More than 75% of all unauthorized immigrants have lived in the United States for more than ten years. These people have lived and worked in our country and have become integrated into their communities, as has been repeatedly demonstrated by the organized local citizen actions against deportations of these community members.

As the Brookings study confirms, without authorized status and documentation, foreign-born residents likely have little bargaining power in the workforce and are exposed to a higher risk of mistreatment. The study also found:

- Eighty percent of immigrants today come from Asia or Latin America, while in 1910, more than 80% of immigrants came from Europe.
- Immigrants are much more likely than others to work in construction or service occupations, but children of immigrants work in roughly the same occupations as the children of natives.

- Immigrants contribute positively to government finances over the long run, and high-skilled immigrants make especially large contributions.
- Immigration in the United States does not increase crime rates. Immigrants to the United States are considerably less likely than natives to commit crimes or to be incarcerated, but restricting access to legal employment for unauthorized immigrants leads to an increased crime rate.

In addition, the Brookings report notes: "The intensity and form of detention and deportation actions has changed substantially over the past few years and requires further research."

Questions are sometimes asked (or accusations leveled) relating to the use of government-paid services by undocumented immigrants. The Department of Homeland Security found that 15.5% of undocumented immigrants benefit from Medicaid; a total of 16.1% of native-born Americans used Medicaid. Around $2 billion a year goes to hospitals that must care for anyone who shows up at the emergency room. The study found that 9.1% of undocumented immigrants used food stamps, compared to 11.6% of native-born citizens.

In addition, almost half of all undocumented immigrants, 3.4 million people, pay Social Security payroll taxes. In 2010, they and their employers contributed $13 billion. They do so even though they are not eligible for Social Security benefits upon retirement. Use of welfare is negligible, less than 1%, for both populations.

One rationale for tight immigration policies sometimes offered is as a means to prevent terrorism.

Links Between Terrorism and Migration, a report from the International Centre for Counter-Terrorism, concludes that tighter migration control might hurt bona fide migrants, asylum seekers, and legal foreign residents while being limited and not very effective at stopping those with evil intentions.

America does not have a "good" record with respect to immigrants over the years.

The enslavement and continued fiscal and social discrimination against the African American population by those with European roots is well documented, as is their decimation of Native Americans. As James Woods notes in his *New Yorker* article about de Tocqueville's 1831 visit and subsequent book, "Nothing is subjected to angrier analysis in *Democracy in America* than those two great wounds in nineteenth-century American society: the institution of slavery and the steady eviction and extermination of the Indian tribes."

There has also been a pattern of discrimination that seemed to fit each immigrant group in the 19th and into the 20th century. Be they the Italians, the Irish, or the Jews, the first generation of immigrants (those grandparents mentioned earlier) tended to settle in housing enclaves and to have more problems getting jobs and buying homes. Their children, the first generation born in the country, then got educated, got jobs, and moved out of their ethnic ghetto. In fact, many of the same neighborhoods in big cities served each of these populations in turn. That pattern broke down with the "up-migration" of African Americans from the South into northern and western cities in the 20th century, where they moved in to the same ethnic-serving neighborhoods, but the next generation did not have the same opportunities to move to better city neighborhoods or suburbs.

A much stronger application of discrimination unfolded in the United States with respect to two Asian populations: the Chinese and the Japanese. For most of those years, San Francisco was at least partially in sync with the rest of the country, even as some greater openness to Asian and then Latino immigration could be found in the Bay Area.

Chinese Migrants in the United States

During the first modern-day Chinese immigration to North America, in the mid-19th century, Chinese immigrants were tolerated by the local white people on the West Coast for the large unskilled labor force they provided. Yet as it became harder to mine for gold and more people flooded in, the tide turned, and animosity increased toward the Chinese. It was a hostility that would become part of the landscape for at least the next hundred years.

The Chinese miners were gradually driven away from the mining camps, sometimes by physical force, sometimes by claim-jumping, and more officially with the assistance of California state legislators using various techniques including the Foreign Miners Tax. The tax, enacted in 1850, levied a 20-dollar-a-month tax on foreigners from Asia and Mexico. It was repealed in 1851, but then re-enacted in 1852 with a three-dollar-per-month tax.

California governor John Bigler blamed the Chinese for causing a depression in wages, and in 1852, he called for immigration restrictions. Several state bills were passed relating to limits on Chinese migrants, but these limits were mostly nullified because of treaties between the two countries.

The post–Civil War economy fell into decline in the 1870s, leading to the Panic of 1873 and a subsequent six-year economic depression. Anti-Chinese animosity became more strongly focused and politicized, led by people such as Denis Kearney.

Kearney, himself an Irish immigrant, helped build a group of unemployed laborers into the Workingman's Party of California. Part of his platform focused on antipathy to Chinese workers, blaming them, as scapegoats, for the problems of white workers, even though there were only 63,000 Chinese in the country in 1870 out of a population of 39 million. This antipathy, pushed by West Coast politicians and by union labor leaders, culminated in the 1882 Chinese Exclusion Act, the first legislation to place broad restrictions on immigration to the United States. The act was renewed for a second ten-year term and was then made permanent with the addition of registration and certification of residency requirements, lasting until its repeal in 1943 as a result of the World War II US alliance with China.

In order to gain admission, or more often re-admission, to the country after passage of the Exclusion Act, about 10,000 Chinese appealed the restrictions in

federal court between 1882 and 1905 by way of a petition for habeas corpus. Initially, for the most part the US
courts ruled in favor of the petitioner. Successful cases
were based either on loopholes in the law, existing international treaties, or such reasonable judicial observa-
tions that it was not possible for people to have re-entry
documents that did not yet exist at the time they temporarily left the country. The Scott Act in 1888 closed off
most of those judicial approvals.

Several illegal processes to get around the Exclusion
Act emerged after the 1906 San Francisco earthquake
and subsequent fire. People could be found to testify
to the birth of a certain youngster to certain parents at
a specific address on a specific date, but whose birth
certificate had burned. Other forged paperwork would
show a claimed relationship to an American citizen, again
in place of "destroyed" documents. The term "paper
sons" was used to describe some of these migrants.

After being forced out of their mines, the Chinese
immigrant miners founded their own enclaves in and
around San Francisco, and took other jobs such as laun-
dry and restaurant work.

Similarly, those who had worked on building the
Union Pacific railroads, and in the mines run by the
railroad, became targets in places like Wyoming after the
tracks were completed, and many headed to the more
densely Chinese-populated San Francisco. The labor
force in California was 20% Chinese by 1870.

Angel Island Immigration Station, now Angel Island
State Park in San Francisco Bay, became a West Coast
immigration processing center from 1910 to 1940. The

center processed over 56,113 Chinese immigrants. More than 30% of those who arrived were sent back.

Hells Canyon Massacre of 1887

Not all hostility to Chinese immigrants played out in the legislatures and the courts.

The Snake River runs down between Oregon and Idaho, serving for a distance as the border between them. The Hells Canyon section of the river reflects the rocky cliffs and white-water rapids of this deepest gorge in North America. This is where 34 Chinese miners were robbed and killed in May 1887.

They were employed by the Sam Yup Company of San Francisco, one of six largest Chinese companies that worked the area beginning in October 1886. The bruised and battered bodies of the miners were found downstream.

While the river rapids and turbulent currents would have thrown and battered the bodies against the rocks, it was confirmed that the Chinese men were shot, and their bodies had been hacked into pieces with axes, before they were thrown into the river.

The bodies of ten victims were identified: Chea-po, Chea-Sun, Chea-Yow, Chea-Shun, Chea Cheong, Chea Ling, Chea Chow, Chea Lin Chung, Kong Mun Kow, and Kong Ngan. The amount of gold stolen from the miners was estimated to be worth between $4,000 and $5,000; the gold was never recovered. A gang of Oregon horse thieves and ranch hands, which included a 15-year-old schoolboy, was suspected for the killings.

The Sam Yup Company of San Francisco hired Lee Loi, who later hired Joseph K. Vincent, a 19th-century Idaho justice of the peace and US commissioner, to head an investigation into the deaths. In March 1888, Frank Vaughan confessed to being part of the massacre and turned state's evidence against the others. A grand jury indicted six Wallowa County, Oregon, men for murder. Hiram Maynard, Hezekiah Hughes, and a schoolboy named Robert McMillan were tried and found innocent. The ringleaders, J. T. Canfield, Homer LaRue, and Bruce Evans, fled Wallowa County and were never caught.

Vincent did submit a report to the Chinese consulate, and he was successful in securing very limited congressional financial compensation to the families.

The site was officially named the Chinese Massacre Cove in 2005, and a three-language memorial plaque was placed there in 2012.

Bubonic Plague in Chinatown

The plague has devastated human societies, in several waves, at least as far back as the Byzantine Empire in the sixth century. The so-called third major plague pandemic erupted in 1855, in China. By the start of the 20th century, infected rats traveling on steamships had carried it to all six inhabited continents; it took 100 years to run its course, claiming an estimated 15 million lives.

In 1894, a Hong Kong–based doctor named Alexandre Yersin identified the *bacillus Yersinia pestis* as the cause of the disease. A few years later, another physician finally confirmed that bites from rat fleas were the main way the infection spread to humans.

Dr. Joseph Kinyoun, who was the founder and first director of the United States' Hygienic Laboratory, the predecessor of the National Institutes of Health, was conducting research on the plague, and tracking its spread through Europe and Asia. He anticipated that the disease would most likely reach the United States on the West Coast, which received heavy ship traffic from Asian cities including those with ongoing epidemics.

In fact, the plague did reach San Francisco in March 1900. A French sailing vessel brought the first deaths from the plague; once it docked, an additional 18 Chinatown residents also succumbed.

People in the Chinatown area were experiencing plague symptoms of fevers, fatigue, swollen lymph nodes, and muscle aches, often followed by meningitis, gangrene, and, for many, death. Even though research at the time had shown it was caused by Yersinia pestis, which was found in small rodents and spread by fleas, more anti-Chinese sentiment spread through the city and all of California. Public blaming of "dirty" Chinese fed further into an acceptance of making racism socially acceptable.

Ultimately, the mayor chose not to inform the public of the outbreak, even after people began to die, because of concerns that it would negatively affect the city's commercial businesses.

Finally, the city was put under quarantine, with all of the sanitary services suspended, until the presence of the pathogens was located. Rather than focusing on the older approach of isolating the ill, Kinyoun supported the Board of Health in "cleaning up" San Francisco's Chinatown through trash removal and rodenticidal fumigation of sewers and houses with sulfur dioxide. A campaign was created to sterilize as much of the city as possible, an almost impossible feat. As more deaths ensued, officials began to patrol the streets looking for anyone with signs of the disease. These patrols further contributed to Chinese residents' distrust of the government.

Injustice against Japanese-Americans

San Francisco's Japantown, known in Japanese as "Nihonmachi," is considered the oldest and largest Japantown in the United States.

When the first group of Japanese immigrants came to San Francisco in the 1860s, they settled in the Chinatown section that was South of Market at the time. After the 1906 earthquake and fire, Japanese families moved a bit further west in the city, to the Western Addition, in an area bordered by Pine Street on the north and by Geary Boulevard on the south.

Entering the 1940s, more than 5,000 Japanese Americans lived in Japantown, and they were served by more than 200 Japanese-owned businesses.

Changes came in 1941 when, on December 7 at 7:55 a.m., Japanese planes attacked the Pearl Harbor naval base in Hawaii, killing 2,400 and wounding 1,200 Americans. On December 8, President Franklin Roosevelt went to the US Congress with a request for a declaration of war on Japan.

Then, on February 12, 1942, Roosevelt signed Executive Order 9066, authorizing the Secretary of War "to prescribe military areas...from which any or all persons may be excluded." The western part of California, from the Oregon border to south of Los Angeles, became identified as Military Area 1. In order to avoid feared "espionage" and "sabotage to national defense," all Japanese and Japanese Americans were then ordered to move to internment camps.

Almost 120,000 people of Japanese descent were driven from their homes and shuttled into residential camps; some 70,000 of them were American citizens. In addition to the Japanese, many of Italian and German descent, as well as Jewish refugees, were also sent to the camps as possible threats to the country based on earlier immigration to the United States.

On the first day of evacuation from Japantown, April 29, 1942, people were allowed to pack just a few of their personal items. The process took them to the Civil Control Station to register before being sent to the Tanforan Assembly center in San Bruno, 12 miles south of San Francisco. It was just one of 17 "civilian assembly centers" designed to process the detention of Japanese Americans for up to six months.

A total of 7,816 people were held at Tanforan from April 28 to October 13, 1942, the second largest assembly center in California. Most of the Japanese who were processed at Tanforan were incarcerated at the Topaz Internment Camp in Utah from 1943 to 1945.

While some of the people were able to return to their homes in Japantown after the war, others relocated to other parts of San Francisco and the Bay Area. Estimates of the value of property confiscated from Japanese Americans ran as high as $400 million.

At the same that the Japanese were in the internment camps, the population of the African American community in San Francisco grew substantially, from 4,836 to 43,460. This influx took place in response to the many wartime jobs that needed to be filled, particularly including shipbuilding at the San Francisco Naval Shipyard. Many of the African Americans who came were looking to escape the Jim Crow laws, a collection of state and local statutes that legalized racial segregation throughout the southern United States.

As there was available housing in the Japantown community, many people moved into the houses. New businesses were founded, changing the makeup of the neighborhood, which further displaced the Japanese when they returned from the camps.

While most people did not believe that those with Japanese ancestry in the country were dangerous or a problem for the war effort, they somehow justified the internment of those with Japanese ancestry because of baseless suspicions of a few members of that community.

In a 1944 documentary film titled *A Challenge to Democracy*, which showed the roundup of Japanese Americans, the narrator states that many Japanese Americans volunteered to fight in the war even while they were at relocation centers, fighting for "American ideals that show democracy, freedom [and] equality of opportunity, regardless of race, creed, or ancestry."

Amazingly though, the federal government still denied the contradiction between their words promoting American idealism and their cruel actions in locking over 100,000 innocent people in camps. The government defended this large-scale, federal racial profiling as a protection of the entire nation, at the expense of a significant number of its own citizens. Studies showed that racially charged post–Pearl Harbor fears and the economic self-interests of agricultural groups who would profit by taking over lands farmed by Japanese Americans played important roles in the calls for removal.

Halfway through the war, a Japanese American military unit was formed, the 442nd Infantry Regiment. The 442nd served in Europe, becoming the most decorated unit in US military history. The related 552nd Field Artillery Battalion helped liberate prisoners from a concentration camp in Dachau. In the Pacific, Japanese Americans who served in the military intelligence unit were part of the Japanese surrender.

It took more than one generation for the Japanese Americans to fully integrate to the country again, with significant roles now at all levels of government and industry.

American Immigration in the 21st Century

Perspectives on immigration continue to be uneven in this 21st century. Issues include what our general immigration policies should be; what we should do about people who got to settle in to homes and work and build families here, but who had arrived illegally; what we should do about people from other countries seeking asylum or refuge here; and how we should treat people who arrive without proper documentation, including those here in search of asylum.

As with so many other issues in the United States at this time, the issues have been significantly polarized politically. A focus on the real issues and needs of people — both people who live and work here legally and those without such status — is attempted here.

America's conflicting values come into play in many cities and towns, where divides within the community run deep. San Francisco values lean strongly toward building and adopting a comprehensive immigration policy that takes the needs of all groups involved into account.

In some towns across the country, the general mood has been that migrants who are here illegally should be sent back "home." Yet those same people often rally to support the families when undocumented immigrants in their own communities are taken from the homes they have lived and worked in for dozens of years, breaking up those families and losing friends and contributing members of the community.

In December 2019, the Burleigh County, North Dakota, commission voted to continue accepting new refugee resettlements. For 2020, this county of 95,000 capped the number of refugees at 25.

A massive 2018 Immigration and Customs Enforcement (ICE) raid changed life in O'Neill, Nebraska, population 2,600. Economically dependent on agriculture, this mostly white town was also the home to scores of Central Americans who had fled poverty and unrest.

O'Neill is a community that was founded in 1875 by an Irish-born general who had fought in the Civil War and who brought three groups of Irish immigrants with him. In 2016, there were 1,500 hundred Latinos living in O'Neill. Buzzfeed reported:

> [the raid] shook long-time residents of O'Neill, a deeply religious, conservative town that voted overwhelmingly for President Trump, exposing fault lines that divided friends who rarely, if ever, spoke about immigration. The immigration status of workers, their effect on the economy, and their place in the community were always assumed but never spoken about.

The migrants predominantly work in local farms and processing plants, while many of the longer-term residents in town work in the local hospital.

One O'Neill farmer's perspective was that the raid was a good thing, feeling that it will send a message to employers to hire authorized workers or get caught. Another resident's perspective was that the agents should have arrested the alleged criminals and helped the workers who were just trying to get by.

The *Intercept* reported on a 2018 ICE raid in Morristown, Tennessee, in which 97 men and women who worked in the plant in that town were detained. As in O'Neill, the community was divided. Were criminals arrested? The *Intercept* noted:

While the raid was prompted by an IRS
investigation of the family-run business,
whose owners were accused of evading
taxes, filing false tax returns, and illegally
employing undocumented workers, so far,
they have not been charged.

The *Intercept* article also reviewed a raid in Pottsville,
Iowa, a town of 2,200, in 2008. Twenty percent of the
town's population was detained that day. The raid was
prompted by fiscal and workplace violations by the
plant's managers, and Sholom Rubashkin, chief executive officer of the Postville plant, was sentenced to 27
years in prison. President Donald Trump commuted his
sentence in December 2017, after he had served eight
years.

In Morton, Mississippi, a town that is 25% Latino, 342
people out of a population of 3,000 were arrested in an
ICE raid in August 2019. This town, which voted roughly
60% Republican in 2016, is also divided in its feelings;
for many, including folks like Cathy Johnson, their view
is clear: "If you're here illegally, you shouldn't be." The
impact of the raids rippled across town, from the fears of
adults to the fragile emotions of children, and also from
banks to churches to shops. One local resident, who
worked at a chicken-processing plant for ten years before opening a small restaurant, reported: "My business
is at 50% now."

The Morton raid was one of six ICE raids in
Mississippi that day. In total, 680 people were detained.
While 271 were released with orders to appear before an

immigration judge, 377 are still in ICE custody. None of the employers at the six companies have been criminally charged or arrested.

Kate Brick, director of state and local initiatives at New American Economy, noted: "Immigrants in Miami are the backbone of the industries that drive growth in the area, from construction to manufacturing." Immigrants make up 62.7% of the city's construction workers and 59% of manufacturing workers, paying more than $16 billion in federal, state, and local taxes in 2017.

Outside the Tyson poultry processing plant in Noel, Missouri, a sign reads, "Now hiring, call today." Some 1,500 employees at the plant come from around the world: Africa, the Pacific, Latin America, and Asia. Locals don't apply.

Across the US, a number of cities have actively supported the welfare of their residents with respect to ICE raids by alerting the residents in advance. These cities include Atlanta, Baltimore, Chicago, Denver, Houston, Los Angeles, Miami, New Orleans, New York, and San Francisco.

Houston mayor Sylvester Turner states:

> It impacts adversely public safety as well. Because we rely upon immigrants and others to report when crimes are being committed in their neighborhoods...and people are shying away from public services.

Denver mayor Michael B. Hancock states:

> We want to reiterate that Denver stands with our immigrant and refugee families, that we do not support family separation or the round-up of immigrant families to spread fear in our community.

Atlanta mayor Keisha Lance Bottoms states:

> We've closed our city detention centers to ICE because we don't want to be complicit in family separation.

Towns like Mount Pleasant, Iowa, where 8% of residents are Latino, many of whom lack papers to live legally in the United States, and Marshalltown, Iowa, which learned from 1996 and 2006 ICE raids, have developed response plans to take care of the children after possible future raids.

The Swift pork processing plant estimated that they lost the $500,000 in production in Marshalltown in 2006, and $50 million nationwide, and that their workforce was depleted in major ways, and remaining workers no longer trusted a management that knew the raids were coming and did not warn them. Homes owned by Latinos lost one-third of their value.

In one immigration hearing for Marshalltown resident Maria Mendoza, community members and organizations presented the judge with 150 letters that spoke to her good character, and three US citizens spoke on her behalf. She was granted residency and the opportunity to apply for citizenship after ten years.

Across the country, undocumented immigrants are our friends and neighbors. They go to our churches; their kids play on sports teams with our kids. They are hardworking, tax-paying, law-abiding residents, not some amorphous mass.

A discussion of immigration at this point in the 21st century involves a disparate range of immigrants: those who come here legally or illegally; those coming to join family members, or for work, or for school; and those coming as refugees or for asylum. The issue of long-term illegal residents, and their children, receives its own attention. Immigration policies have also become increasingly politicized, with rigid positions often ignoring the real economic and social benefits and costs.

The non-partisan Migration Policy Institute's detailed 2019 summary of statistics on immigration since the year 2000 includes:

- The overall immigrant population continues to grow, but at a slower rate than before the 2007–09 recession.
- Recent immigrants are more likely to be from Asia than from Mexico, and are also more likely to have a college degree.
- The size of the unauthorized population appears to be on the decline.
- Deportations from within the United States are rising.
- The United States in 2018 resettled the smallest number of refugees since formal creation of the refugee resettlement program in 1980.

- During the 2000–2017 period, the five states with the largest percent growth of immigrants included North Dakota, Delaware, Tennessee, South Dakota, and Kentucky.
- The five largest states in absolute growth are Texas, California, Florida, New York, and New Jersey.

Looking specifically at those seeing refuge or asylum, the Institute reports that a total of approximately 55,000 people were admitted to the United States in these two categories in 2018:

- In 2018, 22,491 refugees were resettled in the United States, amounting to less than half of the admission ceiling of 45,000 allocated for that year. This represents a 58% drop compared to the 53,716 admitted in 2017.
- 2018 marked the first time the United States lost its top position as the leader in global refugee resettlement in favor of Canada, which resettled about 28,000 refugees.
- In 2018, an estimated 106,147 affirmative asylum applications were received by US Citizenship and Immigration Services (USCIS) — 25% fewer than the 141,695 in 2017. This is the first decline in application volume after eight years of growth.
- According to USCIS, in 2018, 30% of affirmative asylum adjudicated petitions were approved, a decline from the 43% in 2016 and 37% in 2017.
- According to the most recent data available at the time of this writing, in 2017, 26,568 individuals,

including principal applicants and their spouses and/or unmarried children under age 21, were granted asylum after seeking protection upon or after arrival in the United States.

Issues of poverty and drug-based gang violence in Mexico, Central America, and Venezuela have served to increase the numbers of migrants from those areas seeking entry to the United States for asylum. The United Nations Refugee Agency details how organized gangs, called *maras*, have dramatically escalated organized crime in El Salvador, Honduras, and Guatemala. San Salvador, El Salvador; Tegucigalpa, Honduras; and San Pedro Sula, Honduras, are among the ten most dangerous cities in the world, and Honduras is one of the three countries in the world with the highest rate of violent deaths of women. Along with the high rate of brutal homicides, including against women and girls, children in their early teens face forced recruitment into gangs and sexual violence.

As the women who choose to leave make their way north, they are often subjected to further sexual violence, or to being held hostage for ransom, or to also falling victim to human trafficking on their journeys.

Time magazine reported what 15-year-old Maria detailed in her asylum-seeking hearing: "Two years ago, a friend of mine died in a very cold-blooded way. She died cut to pieces. My best friend," Maria said in Spanish, beginning to recount what she told an asylum officer.

As she recalled the story again, Maria's soft voice trembled, and tears spilled down her cheeks. She said police in El Salvador asked her to identify body parts pulled from a bag dumped in a river. She recognized a birthmark on her friend's leg.

"I was traumatized." Maria sobbed. "I still am from seeing that body split apart. That dismembered head. Those arms...As time went by, I didn't want to go out, or eat, or do anything. The only thing I wanted to do was to die. I told myself that the same thing could happen to me."

Two additional factors are currently prominent in an overview of immigration policy.

The first has to do with the ways in which immigration policies are being promulgated and formulated at this time.

The Universal Declaration of Human Rights includes Article XIV, detailing the right to asylum in other countries from persecution. The US Citizenship and Immigration Office website indicates our long-standing rules: "You may apply for asylum if you are at a port of entry or in the United States. You may apply for asylum regardless of your immigration status and within one year of your arrival to the United States."

This long-established process of arriving in the United States without authorization and going directly to Immigration personnel to seek asylum has recently been altered. Crossing the US. border without authorization is now being identified as a misdemeanor crime. Then, that crime is being used to deny asylum authorizations.

Further, a 2018 *Texas Monthly* summary of current procedures for those seeking asylum reads:

> The parents come in and say, "We're per-
> secuted" or give some reason for asylum.
> They come in. And then their child or chil-
> dren are taken away and they're in lockup
> for at least six weeks away from the kids
> and often don't know where the kids are.

There are major concerns about the recent thorough-
ly documented procedures by which children and parents are separated from each other; children are being
incarcerated in prison-like settings with wire fencing and
cement flooring, and records of family separations are
not being kept, so the locations of hundreds of children
are simply unknown by the government, much less the
parents. These violations of human decency and both
national and international values and agreements are
abominable to those holding American values.

Conservatives have pointed out that President
Obama increased enforcement and deportation of undocumented aliens. They skip over several other details.

The first is that the Obama administration worked to
deport such folks who had committed crimes in addition
to the "crime" of having crossed the border.

More significantly, Obama's approach was reaching
out from his side for a comprehensive solution on immigration. Conservatives have accused liberals of not
caring about our immigration rules and laws, or about
having more secure borders. Obama's policies were
an attempt to build a common ground that addressed
both the needs for enforceable and enforced immigration procedures and the needs of the people seeking to

immigrate. He was not met with conservative enlistment into a program that did take all aspects of this complicated issue into account.

One additional factor is that, by whatever name you call it, the current administration is enforcing immigration policies that are based on religious and ethnic discrimination, which violates the values of this country and of the people who claim to love the American ethos.

The second major issue is DACA.

The "Dreamers" — Deferred Action for Childhood Arrivals

In 2012, the Department of Homeland Security (DHS) issued a memo establishing the DACA program. DHS delineated a set of criteria by which "certain young people who were brought to the United States as young children, do not present a risk to national security or public safety, and meet several key criteria" would be able to receive a temporary protection from deportation, for a period of two years, and be eligible to apply for work authorization. Individuals who are eligible are required to complete an application process and undergo a thorough background check, including fingerprinting, and are required to renew their deferred action every two years. DACA eligibility required that youngsters arrived here before 2007 and were below the age of 16 on their arrival. The average DACA recipient arrived in the United States in 1999, when they were just seven years old, and 37% arrived before the age of five.

According to the Center for American Progress, DACA recipients and their households pay $5.7 billion in federal taxes and $3.1 billion in state and local taxes annually. In addition to this, DACA recipients boost Social Security and Medicare through payroll taxes.

In 2018, two-thirds of Americans in an NPR poll agreed that people brought to the United States as children and now residing in the country illegally should be granted legal status.

In 2019, a national poll, commissioned by the Immigration Hub, found immense enthusiasm for putting "Dreamers" and Temporary Protected Status holders onto a path to citizenship. According to that poll, 74% of Colorado voters, 71% of Pennsylvania voters, and 78% of Michigan voters believe that the US government should offer that path.

In Michigan, support stretches across party lines, with 95% of Democrats, 80% of Independents, and 56% of Republicans supporting protections for undocumented immigrant youth and Temporary Protection Status holders, who are unable to return to their home countries due to natural disasters or civil unrest or war. In Pennsylvania and Colorado, the majority of Democrats and Independents also support legalization, while Republicans edge close, at 48% and 47% respectively.

In poll after poll, American voters have shown overwhelming support for legalizing DACA recipients. In one 2017 poll, nearly 90% of respondents across party lines affirmed their support for "a right to residency for undocumented immigrants who arrived in the United States as children."

At this time, there are governmental and judicial processes in place considering the shutting down of the DACA program, and those processes are highly politicized. President Trump has said that he supports the DACA youth. Yet his administration has gone to the Supreme Court asking them to end the program. He has also indicated that he would be willing to open the door to a DACA deal with the Democrats if the Supreme Court shuts it down, effectively using Dreamers as political pawns.

It is also fascinating to note that Trump's appeal to the Supreme Court is based on what he says the previous president did not have the authority to do, even as he claims that the Second Amendment says that he, as president, can do anything he wants.

The question is not supposed to be about who passed or issued which piece of legislation or policy — rather, it is about who these teens and young adults are. They are the kids who grew up here, who went to school here with "our" kids, who are going to college and working and contributing to our society and our economy.

Welcoming the Stranger

American artist Norman Rockwell wrote:

> I'd been reading up on comparative religion. The thing is that all major religions have the Golden Rule in Common. 'Do unto others as you would have them do unto you.' Not always the same words but the same meaning.

Rockwell quoted the wording of that concept from a number of the world's religions, from Christianity to Taoism. Here's a small sampling of the powerful support for this shared worldwide human value:

- Ezekiel, who has been acknowledged as a prophet in Judaism, Christianity, and Islam, is quoted in the Old Testament as saying: "You shall allot it as an inheritance for yourselves and for the sojourners who reside among you and have had children among you. They shall be to you as native-born children of Israel."
- Matthew, author of the first Gospel of the New Testament, quoted Jesus: "For I was hungry and you gave me food, I was thirsty and you gave me drink, I was a stranger and you welcomed me, I was naked and you gave me clothing, I was sick and you took care of me, I was in prison and you visited me."
- According to a tenet in Hindu tradition: "Let a person never turn away a stranger from his house, that is the rule."
- Secular humanist Pablo Neruda said: "To feel the love of people whom we love is a fire that feeds our life. But to feel the affection that comes from those whom we do not know, from those unknown to us, who are watching over our sleep and solitude, over our dangers and our weaknesses — that is something still greater."

Safeguarding Our Children

If you were a Jewish parent in Vienna, Austria, in 1938, would you have been able to put your ten-year-old daughter onto a train to Britain to keep her safe from the Nazis — knowing you would most likely never see her again?

Ilse Hoenigsberg's family did. A survivor, Ilse would later learn that her mother and sister were shipped to Therezin and then Auschwitz, where they were murdered by the Nazis. While her father survived internments, both at Dachau and in Italy, he died before he and his daughter could be reunited.

In today's world, the parallel can be found in Maria's description of the Honduran city of San Pedro Sula, in *Time*:

> [The gang] rules this entire region. At first, they just controlled the drug trade, so if you avoided that you were generally left alone. Over the last few years they have taken over everything. They extort payments from honest businesses. They rob and harass people with no fear of the police. They now control the lives of everyone.

So again, ask yourself how bad things would need to be for you to undertake the journey of hundreds of miles, on foot, across seas, and through untold dangers, to bring yourself and your family to safety? Or, to consider, would you be prepared to send your ten-year-old child on a perilous journey alone, with smugglers, traveling through areas infested with gangs and kidnappers? What kind of reception would you hope to have, for yourself or for your child, upon arrival in a safe country?

Once you've thought about that, try to step away from political perspectives of any slant or bias, and consider the ways that we can best serve both our nation and our own humanity.

This is much broader than simply a "snowflake" liberal position. Grover Norquist, a widely known conservative political economic activist, stated:

> It's not only good policy to have more immigrants in the United States — dramatically more immigrants than we do today, to having a path forward for those people who are here. It's not only a good idea, but it's good politics...I think we need comprehensive reform that deals with the people who've been here for some time...I don't care how tall the fence is as long as the doors are big enough.

The country is still waiting for balanced immigration legislation that provides a reasonable path to citizenship for those undocumented immigrants who have been here making their homes and raising their families, that makes DACA an established law, that welcomes immigrants who bring their skills to our economy, that has a viable and ethically managed program for those seeking asylum, that has guest worker programs for those who want to come for seasonable work and then go back home, and that has enforceable and humane procedures to constrain illegal immigration.

San Francisco values support such a comprehensive immigration package. So do the values of most Americans.

Take Action

1. **A comprehensive immigration policy.** We need legislators from all sides who are willing to work for a comprehensive and balanced solution to immigration issues. Ask your current representatives whether they support such a program, or, if not, why not. Support candidates who are looking for a truly comprehensive solution on this very real human issue, rather than those who only see one small piece of the issue.

2. **Welcoming.** Our culture is built on the broad range of people who came to the country from all over the world. It's a big part of what makes America great. Consider if you found yourself in a new country, torn from the life you had known, how comforting it would be if someone reached out to welcome you, and to help you get settled in your new community. Recognize that you can be that "someone," through such groups as the non-governmental, nonprofit International Rescue Committee.

3. **Racism and bias.** Remember how this country has been biased against so many different groups, religions, and ethnicities over the last

three centuries. Stand tall yourself, and invite and insist that your legislators also stand against immigration policies that are biased on the basis of religion, color, race. Would you have wanted your forebears to have been denied entry to this country because they came from an area not in favor at the time of their arrival? Pay a society free from bias forward.

CHAPTER 8

San Francisco Isn't Perfect: Addressing Our Problems

A homeless veteran should not have to stand at a freeway exit with a cardboard sign. That's not okay.

— *Joe Walsh*

Most of the homeless residents she met in San Francisco were victims of hard times. They were working and then their apartment building got sold to someone, the investor raised the rents, the person couldn't afford it anymore, they couch surfed for a while, and then they hit the streets.

— *Leilani Farha*

Busy Bee, a cleaning services company, undertook a study in 2018 of 40 urban areas across the country to identify the dirtiest cities in the United States. New York City topped the list, with a "dirtiness index" of 428. Los

Angeles ranked second (index: 318). San Francisco came in ninth place (index: 189).

Nonetheless, the *New York Times* set out to identify the dirtiest street in San Francisco. That distinction went to Hyde Street, in the Tenderloin district. Along with piles of poop on the sidewalk, the *Times* reporter found:

> [Blocks] populated with drug addicts and mentally ill residents, many of whom are part of the city's large homeless population. During the day, drug users reportedly host an outdoor market of sorts, selling heroin, crack cocaine, and amphetamines along the sidewalk.

Common National and International Problems

That one paragraph touches on three major American problems: homelessness, drugs, and mental health. Adding the scarcity of reasonably priced housing in cities like San Francisco to that list generates a robust package of major issues facing cities across the country today.

An overarching problem that has arisen across the world in 2020 is the coronavirus pandemic. As has been noted above, the San Francisco Bay area moved forward very swiftly with shelter in place directives, in efforts to control the speed and depth of its spread. With California and Washington leading, many states followed that Bay area model, which, according to early reports, has shown success. In contrast, at the start of April 2020, ten states, each with Republican governors, had not issued such directives. The unfolding of that disease is ongoing at press time, and its aftermath and full story are yet to be written.

Fabled cities and their environs, such as New York, Paris, Rome, London, and San Francisco, have wonderful and exotic characteristics; they also share some of the same problems. Homelessness has emerged as perhaps the most common major contemporary issue.

In the United States, we sometimes refer to home-less people as "sleeping under the bridge." In London, it's called "sleeping rough."

An estimated 726 people died while sleeping rough in England and Wales in 2018 — an average of two people every day. The average age of death was just 45 for men and 43 for women, compared with 76 for men and 81 for women among the rest of the population. A rough sleeper is nine times more likely to commit suicide than the average person. London has about 16% of England's population, but 27% of rough sleepers are in the capital.

There are similar large increases in homelessness in countries across the European continent. In Italy, the issue takes on big proportions as well — in 2014 (the last year for which data is available), over 50,000 people were homeless. Four out of ten homeless people in Italy have been living on the streets for more than four years, and 30% of them were young.

In Japan, more than 90% of homeless people are men. Most are over 50 years of age, with an average pe-riod of living outdoors exceeding four years. One-fourth of them live in Tokyo. Many were caught out when an informal day-labor system that had flourished for about four decades fell apart in a declining economy. For the women, broken marriages and prolonged illness were the major contributing factors.

The Economist wrote about the presence of homelessness in China in 2019, noting that this is a significant change from 30 years ago, when homeless people were a rare sight in China's cities.

Globally, the five cities identified as the "most homeless" — that is, with the highest rates of homelessness — are Manila, New York City, Mumbai, Los Angeles, and Moscow.

While accurate statistics on the problem are hard to gather, it is estimated that roughly 154 million people worldwide are homeless, and that a billion people currently live without adequate shelter.

Heather Knight, a *San Francisco Chronicle* columnist who has been covering homelessness, reports that the city is spending around $300 million a year on the problem. About half goes to supportive housing and the rest goes to administrative support, shelters, and outreach. "Where San Francisco is falling down on the job is in handling the mental health treatment and drug addiction problems," Knight said. "There are not enough spots for either one. Too often at San Francisco General Hospital, people cycle in and out. There is no place for them."

However, Knight says, there is some good news: "The mayor and Board of supervisors have agreed to push a new program called Mental Health S.F. It will focus and create more mental health beds and put a bond on the

November 2020 ballot to fund more case managers. It's a step in the right direction."

Knight notes that San Francisco is not alone in its homeless problems. It stretches along the entire West Coast, including Oregon and Washington. It is just a bigger problem in California, including an equally big problem in Los Angeles.

While the many failed efforts to address these issues have led some to say that the problems are intractable, efforts are ongoing at all levels in the San Francisco Bay Area to make things better.

The Bay Area values optimism, the sense that something can be done, and is willing to put the human and fiscal resources to bear in moving toward creating solutions for homelessness.

Let us examine efforts, in San Francisco and across the country, that are being put forward to deal with these shared problems.

Drug Addiction

The *San Francisco Chronicle* reported that there were about 24,500 injection drug users in the city in January 2019.

A needle exchange program for injection drug users is one program aimed both at health improvement related in particular at HIV and hepatitis C, and at environmental cleanliness in San Francisco. The *San Francisco Examiner* reported that, in 2018, the program distributed 5.8 million syringes and collected 3.8 million, an improved collection rate of about 65%.

Drug-rehabs.com, the website for a national drug treatment group called Addiction Recovery Choice, features an article under the headline, "San Francisco tops list of America's Drug Capitals." The article notes: "The City by the Bay earned the unpleasant distinction of ranking sixth in *Forbes* magazine's list of American cities with the worst drug problem." (The reader might note, with some wry amusement, that for some reason the headline for the article is "San Francisco tops list of America's Drug Capitals.")

Further down, the article goes on to say that "the good news for Bay Area residents and visitors is that there are a number of nationally recognized, highly respected Northern California drug rehab centers in San Francisco and surrounding areas."

George Gáscon, San Francisco's District Attorney until the summer of 2019, has long fought a battle to decriminalize drug possession and use. In his wide-ranging search for a solution, he studied the vast improvements in health and public safety since drugs were decriminalized in Portugal as one innovative approach.

In Oakland, Highland Hospital is among a small group of institutions that have begun to initiate opioid addiction treatment right in their emergency rooms. In San Francisco, city health workers are proactively seeking homeless people with opioid use disorder and offering them buprenorphine prescriptions on the spot, in the streets. Used to treat narcotics dependence and addiction, buprenorphine helps prevent withdrawal symptoms caused by stopping other opioids.

Meanwhile, emergency specialist Dr. Jennifer Brokaw noted that methamphetamine emergency room visits have soared in San Francisco, from 150 in 2008 to 2,000 in 2016, and deaths from meth have become more frequent than those from opiates.

The American Civil War was the first war where the newly discovered painkiller morphine was used. Opiate addiction became rampant, with easy availability for hundreds of thousands of addicted war veterans. It was also reported that many rural housewives became addicted as a response to the monotony of life in the middle of nowhere. In the last third of that century, one could purchase morphine and heroin with syringes from Sears and Roebuck catalogs.

The arrival of crack cocaine in the mid-1980s offered poor people a cheap alternative to alcohol. Health care consultant Stephen F. Jencks estimates that, by 1991, roughly 30% of all homeless single adults used crack regularly. Heavy drug use can readily lead to homelessness, as marginally employable adults may choose to spend their limited income on drugs instead of rent. Conversely, people who become homeless may become addicts as they become exposed to drugs in shelters and public parks.

San Francisco is smack in the middle of the nation on this issue. Half of the cities and just under half of rural communities across the country identify drug addiction as a top-tier problem, and a third of adults in suburban areas also consider addiction as a major concern.

In August 2019, San Francisco announced the start of a year-long crackdown on drug trafficking as part of an effort to clean up the Tenderloin section of the city. A team drawing together the efforts of 17 law enforcement agencies has been gathered for this effort.

Unaffordable Housing

As *San Francisco Chronicle* columnist Kevin Fisher-Paulson notes: "You cannot fix complex problems with a sledgehammer. Bullying won't fix homelessness. These are individuals living on the streets, human beings with complex issues of addiction, income inequality and mental illness."

Housing is a complex problem, one that includes concerns about the availability or vacancy rates, the costs of owning or renting in the Bay Area, and several tiers of homelessness.

One way in which the San Francisco Bay Area differs from most of the country is the very high cost of owning a home. The Bay Area includes 11 of the 25 most expensive zip codes in the country — with an average home price of $3,385,000.

While the cost of homes in California has tended to be higher than in other parts of the country, that differential has increased significantly over the past 40 years. In 1980, the median home value in the United States was $47,200; the median home price in Palo Alto was $148,900, three times the national average. In 2019, the median home price in the United States had risen to $347,000; in Palo Alto, it was $3,385,000 — ten times the national average.

This price differential is reflected in rents as well. While California salaries tend to be somewhat higher than in most parts of the country, the salary differential does not balance the higher cost of housing.

The average San Francisco apartment is 747 square feet, and the average 2019 rent for an apartment that size was $3,703 a month. Parallels have been drawn between Oakland, California, just across the bay from San Francisco, and Brooklyn, New York, just outside of Manhattan. In both cases, rents in the central city have pushed many people out, and into the neighboring areas. The average rent in Oakland is $2,953. In San Jose, $2,762. In Daly City, $2,629.

In Chicago, the average rent is $1,998. In Houston, $1,101. In Denver, $1,673. In Atlanta, $1,485. In Seattle, $2,122. In Omaha, $929. In Oklahoma City, the average rent is $774.

The higher cost of Bay Area housing and living generates multiple problems. Middle-class service providers, such as teachers, cops, and firefighters, tend to need to buy their housing up to 100 miles outside of the metropolitan area, rather than living in the communities they serve. And lower-earning workers, such as restaurant and hotel staff, often work two or three jobs to be able to afford rent within a two-hour manageable commute to work.

High salaries in the tech industries have enabled employees in those enterprises to live in San Francisco, paying higher rents, gentrifying communities, and reducing the availability of lower rental units. Additionally, San Francisco, like all of California, has simply not built enough new housing to provide shelter for the continued influx of people wanting to live and work here.

California has been investigating ways to rein in rent increases for those who want to live in San Francisco, Los Angeles, and other major cities in the state. Governor Gavin Newsom signed a 2019 law that limits rent increases to 5% for each year plus inflation through January 1, 2030. It also stops landlords from forcing out people without cause in order to raise the rent for new tenants. Oregon is the only other state with state-wide rent control. The California legislature is also working to constrain local community zoning laws in order to allow denser housing construction plus shopping amenities near transportation stations, in an attempt to increase the housing supply.

While the high price of housing, by itself, is not the cause of homelessness, it does contribute to that problem.

One intermediate solution that some Bay Area employees have developed in response to the lack of affordable housing is to live in recreational vehicles (RVs), that is, making a trailer or RV their homes. Instead of moving to Sacramento and commuting three hours a day to get to a low-paying job, they live in a portable home in the Bay Area.

But the RVs need to park someplace, and there are some residents who don't like the lineup of RVs along their streets.

A few cities have opened up unused parking lots and allow these folks to have a permanent location. Oakland is one of the first cities in the Bay Area that has opened its heart to RV dwellers and given them a safe and permanent place to be. But the scarcity of available land,

and the "not in my backyard" mentality constrain this approach.

RV parking centers are designed to solve some of the problems associated with RV living. Oakland created a test location that offers installed portable toilets and wash stations, and the security of a full-time on-site manager; they also made a deal with a company that will bring by mobile shower trucks on certain days during the week.

Oakland claims that this is the first phase of an approach to deal with people living around the city and even helping those who live on the street. They are looking at more locations around the city and have identified the cost at about $150,000 for the new site and $600,000 a year to maintain.

"We have a neighborhood in East Oakland that has been disproportionately impacted by RV dwellers, but we want to be both effective and compassionate as we address the crisis of homelessness in our city," Oakland mayor Libby Schaaf says. "We do not find it acceptable for people to use our sidewalks as trash cans, to put their raw human waste in our storm drain systems. However, we cannot afford to just push this problem somewhere else."

When "B" was hired to build Escondido Village graduate housing at Stanford University, it forced him to consider how he was going to get from his home in Martinez to Palo Alto daily. He decided he would get an RV and live in that during the week. For the weekends, though, he drives 65 miles to his home in Contra Costa County.

"A" is a contractor who parks his RV along El Camino Real next to Stanford property as his temporary address. He has worked on projects for several Bay Area clients, including Santa Clara University, Facebook, and Apple. However, he lives in Fresno with his wife and four of their six children.

Like "B" and other laborers, "A" travels home on the weekends to be with his family, while the RV serves as his home during the week. He drives around to find the closest spot for his job. "I park in Palo Alto, Mountain View, Redwood City...I'm parking everywhere," he said. He said that the jobs pay more in the Bay Area and that allows him to pay his mortgage in Fresno and take care of his family.

Living in an RV could be considered as semi-homelessness. Living in one's car is one step lower on the scale. Sleeping rough — living on the streets, in doorways or makeshift tents — is the more pervasive and difficult problem.

Chronic Homelessness

Homelessness today is often described in three categories:

- Situational or transitional homelessness occurs when a person is forced into homelessness for a short period due to a life crisis, such as job loss, domestic violence, or a natural disaster.
- Episodic or cyclical homelessness is used to describe those who fall in and out of being homeless, oftentimes due to mental illness or addiction.

- Chronic homelessness usually occurs when a person doesn't have the financial or social resources to change their living situation or has an ongoing mental health or addiction issue.

Sadly, in the 21st century, chronic homelessness is on the rise.

Homelessness has been documented in America since 1640, with several major waves since then — from the panhandlers of the 1830s to the "Hoovervilles" of the Great Depression.

During the 1820s and 1830s, with the Industrial Revolution, people began migrating from farms to cities in search of work. Philadelphia and New York had many people walking the streets, leading to the country's first panhandling ordinances. City jails became de facto shelter systems.

The 1850s brought the first documented cases of homeless youth, many of whom were kicked out of their homes because their families could no longer afford to raise them.

The 20th century saw major unemployment during the decade-plus depression that began with the stock market crash of 1929. Enclaves of cardboard and scrap metal shelters, shantytowns called "Hoovervilles," in reference to President Hoover (who was president when the market crashed and is often blamed for the onset of the Depression), were built by the homeless of that era.

Stanford Professor Daniel Weinberger reported that:

> In the early 1990s, the poor constituted 14.5% of the total American population — approximately 40 million citizens. Many of these people were actually part of the underpaid workforce.

Weinberger also noted that the 1990s "witnessed the largest income gap between rich and poor since at least 1947 when statistics started being kept." In addition, there are "persisting gaps between blacks, whites, and Latinos in how they experience poverty and, in many instances, in how society treats the poor in these different communities."

There has also been a dramatic increase in the number of women and children now living in poverty in the United States, with one in four of children under the age of six currently living below the poverty line. Since the mid-1970s, for the first time in United States history, American society has witnessed the emergence of a "class" of homeless people.

One-third of all Americans — 78 million people — are "shelter poor," meaning that they have to spend so much on housing they lack sufficient income to pay for other basic necessities.

Mental illness among individuals has impacted the rise in the number of homeless people in America. Clearly, the structural problems created by de-institutionalization and similar policies throughout the 1980s are at the root of this factor. State-run mental hospitals had quite often served simply as warehouses for discarded human beings, and better solutions for the mentally ill were needed. Even in states with good intentions of providing community-based housing and support services, plans were rarely implemented. Jencks noted: "The mental health policies of limiting involuntary commitment and allowing state hospitals to discharge patients with nowhere to go were a complete disaster."

By 1987, there were 100,000 homeless working-age Americans with mental problems so severe that they could not hold a job. It has been estimated by clinicians that about a third of today's homeless population have "severe" mental disorders.

Although an estimated 15% of homeless people do have jobs, they simply don't earn enough to afford housing.

To meet the federal definition for affordable housing, rent for a one- or two-bedroom apartment must not cost more than 30% of a person's income. Yet in every state, more than the national minimum wage is required to afford an apartment by these criteria, according to a report by the US Conference of Mayors. The US Department of Housing and Urban Development (HUD) estimates that five million US households either pay more than half of their income in rent or live in severely substandard housing.

Needing to spend that much of limited monthly income on rent generates additional problems. Choices need to be made on whether to buy increasingly expensive drugs or food. The term "food insecurity" has come into use to describe people who cannot be sure of having needed minimum food daily.

Nearly 8% of Americans 60 and older were "food insecure" in 2017, according to a recent study released by the anti-hunger group Feeding America. That's 5.5 million seniors who don't have consistent access to enough food for a healthy life.

HUD reported that problem is most acute in parts of the South and Southwest. Louisiana has the highest rate among states, with 12% of seniors facing food insecurity. Memphis fares worst among major metropolitan areas, with 17% of seniors unsure of their next meal.

The Older Americans Act was passed in 1965 and amended in 1972 to provide for home-delivered and group meals for those over the age of 59. Funding has lagged behind population growth and inflation. Adjusting for inflation, funding has dropped by 8% over the past 18 years. Group meals and home-delivered meals have dropped by 21 million in the past 14 years, with only 17% of those who are food insecure getting any meal services under the program.

Seven percent of white seniors in America are food insecure, as are more than 17% of black seniors and 16% of Hispanic seniors.

In 1998, reporters Matthew Robinson and Brian C. Anderson, writing for the conservative *Manhattan Institute Quarterly*, encapsulated the argument that homelessness is not a result of an inadequate housing supply. Rather, they blame the homeless themselves, describing their "choice" of being homeless as self-destructive behavior.

Under the George W. Bush administration, the federal government invested in extensive research and formulated a plan to end to homelessness in ten years. Inspired by this plan, the US Interagency Council on Homelessness and President Bush encouraged cities and communities across the United States to make their own plans to end chronic homelessness, with the help of financing from the federal government. Due to this effort, a lot of cities did see a decrease in their chronic homeless population. But not one city was able to eliminate homelessness.

One major cause for people to become homeless is job loss. Statistics show that 26% of the homeless are people who were working full-time, but who had no resources when they lost their job. They couldn't pay their rent, maybe sold their car, and then just had no place to go.

Substance abuse generates some 18% of homelessness. In some cases, while people may not have been on drugs in the beginning, the drugs helped alleviate the pain and reality of being on the street.

In other circumstances, personal relationships could have been a cause, such as someone being kicked out of their house, mental illness, or divorce.

One of the many unpleasant issues with homelessness on the streets is human feces. Just in 2018, San Francisco had more than 80 calls a day complaining of human feces on the thoroughfares and sidewalks.

In Los Angeles, it was found that there were nine public toilets available in their Skid Row section for some 2,000 homeless people. Aside from the unpleasantness of it, the situation creates a context for the growth of infectious diseases.

Reverend Andrew Bales of the Union Rescue Mission in Los Angeles learned of this the hard way. As he was doing outreach work in the area, an open wound of his came in contact with human waste. The consequent infection led to the amputation of his leg.

While more public toilets can help, people don't necessarily use them, as they are afraid of being robbed or attacked in the restrooms at night.

Both Los Angeles and San Francisco extended their public Pit Stop bathroom programs; paid staff maintain cleanliness and provide security for safety. Mayor Breed stated that when people have access to a clean, safe restroom, they will use it.

In LA, a single Pit Stop site, with toilets, handwashing stations, and an attendant, costs $339,000 a year. It would cost about $450,000 per unit in California to build affordable subsidized housing.

The homeless tent cities create about six tons of garbage every day, and that includes injection needles. Some of these needles still have blood and heroin in them. The smell around these encampments is a stench that lasts for hours.

Some say that the San Francisco Bay Area homeless problem was brought on itself because the society stopped enforcing laws that make it illegal to sleep on the streets. The hard-nosed legal approach, however, has not worked to relieve homelessness in those cities applying it.

It is indeed true that not all who are out there want to come in from the streets. For some, there is a large voluntary component, a choice that they make.

Jeff, standing outside the city's latest shelter proto-type, known as a Navigation Center, says that he was offered housing four times but always turned it down. He could come off the streets if he wanted to, he says — but he didn't want to give up drugs.

Vanessa, a heavily mascaraed transgendered woman, came to San Francisco from Denver a year ago at the invitation of a friend because "everyone comes here." Though she has been attacked and her tents burned, she still lives at the Willow Alley encampment rather than accept housing.

Her fellow camper Susan explains: "Teams come to talk to us, but they can only do so much." Susan has been taken to a Navigation Center, but it felt like a jail. "I'm claustrophobic," she says. The Navigation Centers are designed to be maximally accommodating, but not everyone wants to be accommodated the same way.

In the Bay Area, the notion is that it is being compassionate toward the homeless that allows them to live freely on the street. Yet there are many very caring people who would say allowing people to degenerate on the street is hardly compassionate. What has resulted has created misery and squalor and the cost of taking care of these people has skyrocketed.

Research shows that criminalization of homelessness increases, rather than decreases, homelessness. What's more, the Ninth US Circuit Court of Appeals has ruled, based on a Boise, Idaho case, that cities can't prosecute people for sleeping on the street if they have no other option because it would violate the Constitution's prohibition on cruel and unusual punishment.

Solving Homelessness: A Work in Progress

San Francisco's long-term homeless population remained relatively small through the 1970s. "We didn't even call them homeless people," recalls journalist Steve Talbot, a longtime city resident. In the early 1980s, though, homelessness became a full-blown crisis throughout the country, the result of a combination of massive state and federal cuts to mental health services and public housing, a wave of Vietnam veterans in need of help, skyrocketing home prices, and a spike in unemployment caused by the national recession.

San Francisco mayors have indeed tried, in administration after administration, to address the problem. KQED Radio traced these attempts with a detailed timeline that included:

> ➤ 1982–88: Mayor Dianne Feinstein relied primarily on church-based emergency shelters, soup kitchens, and city-funded overnight stays in cheap, private hotels. The strategy proved costly and, ultimately, unsuccessful.
>
> ➤ 1988–92: Mayor Art Agnos unveiled his "beyond shelter" strategy, a sweeping initiative to provide services to the city's homeless that he claimed would be a model for the nation, where homeless clients could be assessed and receive health and counseling services. His string of shelters opened hastily in 1990 to accommodate victims of the

October 1989 Loma Prieta earthquake, but lacking adequate resources, they soon became overcrowded and understaffed.

➢ 1992–96: Mayor Frank Jordan instituted his Matrix program, an enforcement-based strategy using police to forcibly clear homeless people from the streets and steer them into health and housing services. Without enough services in place to handle the uptick in numbers, though, little progress was made in preventing the homeless from returning to the streets.

➢ 1996–2004: Mayor Willie Brown pledged to bring in outside government funding to expand social services and develop a regional plan with other Bay Area cities, but those plans fell short. Brown did lead a successful increase in the city's affordable housing stock, creating thousands of new units and beds by leasing and renovating cheap residential hotels and heavily subsidizing the rent. During his second term, Brown famously declared homelessness a problem "that may not be solvable." In 2002, the San Francisco's homeless population spiked at more than 8,600, as the city became gripped by a housing shortage and skyrocketing costs amid the economic boom.

➢ 2004–2010: Gavin Newsom championed a "Care Not Cash" measure, slashing cash payments to the homeless and redirecting funds toward housing. In his first year as mayor, he introduced an ambitious ten-year plan to end chronic homelessness by creating 3,000 housing units with supportive services and replacing emergency shelter beds with 24-hour clinics. Although the plan fell short of its goal, it did move thousands of homeless people off the streets over the next decade. After the program's first year, homelessness in the city dropped by nearly 30% from its 2002 high. But then the numbers froze — at about 6,000 people — through the remainder of his tenure. Homelessness, he later claimed, is the "manifestation of complete, abject failure as a society. We'll never solve this at City Hall."

➢ 2011–2017: Mayor Ed Lee opened the city's first Navigation Center, a 24-hour multiservice homeless shelter providing housing assistance and drug abuse rehabilitation, in 2015. A month into his second full term, Lee announced a new city-wide homeless department, an effort to group all services under one roof and spend at least $1 billion over the following four years to help thousands of people find supportive housing. The department launched in July 2016. A year later, it reported a double-digit decrease in family and youth homelessness, but a slight rise in the number of single homeless adults. Lee then launched a "coordinated entry" initiative to consolidate the dozens of city-funded homeless service groups under one system and have a shared database. Meanwhile, public complaints about encampments, human waste, and needles increased sharply, from about 6,300 in 2011 to more than 44,000 in 2016.

➤ 2018–forward: Mayor London Breed entered office pledging to further the reach of programs established by her predecessor. Early on, she committed to adding at least 1,000 new shelter beds by 2020 and upheld Lee's promise of building 5,000 units of housing annually. Her administration added nearly 300 shelter beds, with proposals for about 500 more, and helped move some 1,500 people off the streets. Nevertheless, a one-night homeless count in January identified nearly 9,800 homeless people in San Francisco (including those in jails, hospitals, and rehabilitation facilities) — a 30% increase since 2017.

Some of Breed's efforts to build new shelters hit major roadblocks. Most notably, her plan to build a $4 million, 200-bed Navigation Center on the Embarcadero during the summer of 2019 became tied up in litigation after a "not in my backyard" neighborhood group spent more than $250,000 on a suit to halt construction. The city won in court and moved forward, with the first residents arrived before the end of December 2019. Mayor Breed has put much of her political capital into this specific center, saying, in typical Bay Area style, "Go big, or go home."

Elsewhere in the Country

How have other metropolitan areas addressed homelessness?

In Birmingham, Alabama, Mayor Bernard Kincaid assembled a mayor's commission to develop a ten-year plan to prevent and end chronic homelessness. Some services were offered, but there was no successful elimination of homelessness. In a January 2012 survey, volunteers for One Roof found a total of 1,707 homeless individuals in the Birmingham area. Of those, 662 were residing in transitional shelters, and 347 were sleeping in emergency shelters, leaving 698 unsheltered homeless living on the streets. Among those unsheltered, 347 were considered "chronically homeless."

In St. Louis, Missouri, Toni Wade, a veteran of industry and real estate investing, created Project Outreach, a non-profit agency dedicated to cutting homeless rates among local youth aging out of foster care, veterans, and those previously incarcerated. The agency's goal is to not only house the homeless, but also give them the resources and skills to retain and invest in their own housing. The first phase is focused on providing stable housing for ex-convicts. The project is relatively new and ongoing, with success yet to be measured.

We can see real success in at least one city: Rockford, Illinois. In 2015, Rockford hit a milestone in its battle against homelessness, when it became the first city in the country to effectively end homelessness among military veterans. Among the cornerstones of its approach, Rockford adopted a "housing first" strategy and placed a priority on outreach and relentless public oversight.

Rockford's success actually brought a new influx of homeless veterans to the city, said Brittney Hensley, outreach social worker for the Department of Veteran Affairs. All of them were housed quickly. A moderate-sized city with a population close to 150,000 people,

Rockford then addressed the chronic homeless. They were successful again, as they achieved functional zero for chronic homeless. The city has now moved on to focus on homeless youth, working with the same plan and strategy.

The Navigation Centers in the San Francisco Bay Area are designed to utilize some of the same approach taken by Rockford — to provide individualized services to help get and keep homeless people off the streets.

Along with homelessness, drug problems, housing costs, and mental illness, cities across the country face such issues as on-time and crime-free transportation systems, environmental management, under-funded retirement obligations, and public education.

San Franciscans are upbeat and optimistic. They invest, emotionally and financially, in programs and projects that might possibly be successful in addressing and mitigating these seemingly intractable problems. They look to successful programs, whether from other cities, like Rockford, or other eras, like Roosevelt's Civilian Conservation Corps, in search of approaches that might work.

In these efforts, Bay Area values and American values are, once again, in sync.

Take Action

1. **Recognition.** Homelessness is a pervasive problem, not limited to any locale. Rural and suburban towns and smaller cities have the problem as well as big cities. Homeless people can be anyone, including our former neighbors, co-workers, friends,

and family members. They are individual human beings, not an amorphous mass. Recognize them as individuals, and recognize the problem as a major one for our society.

2. **Be part of the solution.** Consider volunteering at a food pantry or shelter. Support municipal-level to state and national comprehensive efforts to mitigate the problem in ways that are fair and firm but not punitive, and ask those seeking your vote how they are committed to help.

3. **Reject "NIMBYism."** Acknowledging the problem while saying, "Not in my backyard" won't do it. Help support the creation of comprehensive solutions in all neighborhoods — which means being open to having Navigation Centers and subsidized housing in your own backyard.

4. **Mental health.** Adequate public approaches to addressing severe mental health issues have been missing in the country for at least the past 40 years, and the warehousing approach for the mentally ill that we used before that wasn't acceptable either. Seek officials with constructive comprehensive approaches, and support their efforts, including a willingness to spend the money that is necessary.

CHAPTER 9

San Francisco's Political Voices

Where do you get your information from?
— *Congresswoman Anna Eshoo*

With more than 325 million people, the United States is the third most populous country in the world, and also the third largest in area. We are a diverse group, living in cities, suburbs, small towns, on farms, reservations, and in forests. Some of us can trace our roots in the country back a few hundred or even several thousand years, some of us are first- or second-generation Americans, and some have only been here for several months.

Our values have evolved from an amalgamation of the cultures of the many countries our ancestors left in order to come here. We adapt and modify and seek commonality in our values, and in defining who we want to be as a nation.

To meaningfully express our values when we go to the polls, the fundamental question to be addressed is: Who do we aspire to be? Do we want to be a collection of isolated and antagonistic groups wrapped around conflicting ideologies? Do we want to try to return to some earlier period of our history, in which one small group or class of people determined how all of us would live? Or can we identify some values that we hold in common, and find ways of building a governance system that encompasses those values, while at the same time recognizing and supporting individual concerns and interests?

Nancy Pelosi

Nancy Pelosi embodies San Francisco values. Her interpersonal skills and effectiveness in office embodies the heart and soul of a dedicated citizen of the nation. As Speaker of the House of Representatives, she is politically the most powerful woman in the United States. She believes we can and do come together when it matters.

As Speaker, she has forcefully stood for maintaining the role of Congress as one of three co-equal branches of government.

She has spoken of the gracious welcome she received from George W. Bush at the first meeting they had in the Oval Office. She and he went on to work together on major projects, even as they were in strong disagreement about the war that he and his vice president initiated.

She has also spoken of how she and the senior Bush, President George H. W. Bush, were on opposite sides of the discussion of the best way the country should respond to China's Tiananmen Square massacre, yet how they were able to work together to help San Francisco deal with the aftermath of the 1989 Loma Prieta earthquake. She has stood strong in opposition to some of President Trump's initiatives and actions. Yet she answered a reporter's question about hating him angrily, saying that she did not hate him or anyone. She added that she does pray for him regularly.

Nancy Pelosi fundamentally believes that people care about the nation, and that the capacity to respect each other, and to work together on common problems, is not lost.

She also knows in order to get something done to affect these values, it takes guts and grit to effect change.

She learned early on from her father, who served as a congressman from Maryland and then as mayor of Baltimore, that in government, you need to know what power you have and how to use it. She also learned that "the reputation of power is power," and she became expert at counting the votes that are there and those that are perhaps reachable.

Pelosi is an effective organizer and an extremely good listener. She attributes those skills to having successfully mothered five daughters, developing systems to get them all organized, learning how to listen and keep confidences private, and also learning when to intervene and when to let things unfold on their own.

Her savvy, her effectiveness at raising support for members of the House across the country, and her ability to listen to the diverse membership of her party vaulted her over others on the climb up the leadership ladder.

Pelosi was elected speaker after the 2006 midterms. She demonstrated her leadership skills in the battle to save the American economy, where she brought the votes to President George W. Bush to bail out the banks in the financial meltdown in 2008, and once again when she engineered the passage of the breakthrough Affordable Care Act in 2010.

She is not without enemies and detractors. During the 2018 election campaigns, Republicans ran 137,000 negative ads across the country specifically targeting her. True to her power and convictions, these ads didn't faze her, and she went on to secure, once more, her role as Speaker.

At the same time, the reader will recall that, when the coronavirus was first making its way across the country in early 2020, Senate Majority Leader Mitch McConnell sat back, and even started to put the Senate on vacation; Washington waited while Nancy Pelosi negotiated the first bail-out bill with a member of the Trump administration. Only after that bill was negotiated successfully did Mr. Trump and Mr. McConnell sign on and approve that legislation. Pelosi's House of Representatives then went on to negotiate additional bail-out and stimulus bills to address the economic problems of the citizens of the country as well as the corporate interests.

If you should continue to doubt her mastery as a leader, perhaps you might ask yourself: If Nancy Pelosi is as faulty and "out of touch" as her critics say, why are Republicans so bent on undercutting her? Might it be that they are trying to destroy her "reputation of power" — or, perhaps, her extremely effective use of power for the good of the nation?

As her daughter, Christine wrote in her book, *The Nancy Pelosi Way*:

> Nancy loves representing San Francisco and says of the ads dismissing her and her city: "To those who mock me for having *San Francisco Values,* which is their code for being pro-LGBTQ, I say, 'We don't tolerate our differences—that's condescending. We take pride in our diversity. And when it comes to full social equality, the inconceivable to you is the inevitable to us. Listen to what we say because pretty soon you'll be saying it too.'"

For all the barriers she has broken, for all the passion she incites on both sides, Nancy Pelosi did not manage to make the cover of a national newsmagazine, even when she was the first woman Speaker of the House. *Ms.* magazine did feature her on their cover in 2011, naming her as "The Woman TIME & NEWSWEEK Won't Put on Their Covers."

Finally, *Time* put her on their cover, for the first time, in September 2018, with a headline that, appropriately enough, read: "The persistence of Nancy Pelosi."

Other Notable Bay Area Politicians

In San Francisco politics, as summarized by the *Los Angeles Times*, "Liberal" means "middle of the road" and "Progressive" is the leftier label. Nancy Pelosi does, indeed, personify San Francisco's liberal values. Some other notable Bay Area politicians reflect, as well, the range of the region's generally left-of-center approaches to American governance.

Here's a brief introduction to several of them, including Governor Newsom, Senators Feinstein and Harris, Representatives Lee and Speier, Mayors Breed and Schaaf, as well as Jerry Brown, Barbara Boxer, and Willie Brown.

- **Gavin Newsom** served as San Francisco's mayor from 2004–2011 and as lieutenant governor under Jerry Brown from 2011–2019, and he is now the governor of California. He is known to act decisively on issues of fairness without fear of possible political consequences. As has been noted, as mayor, he directed the San Francisco County Clerk to begin issuing marriage licenses to same-sex couples in 2004. During a strike by hotel workers against a dozen San Francisco hotels that was the culmination of two years without a contract and with strikes and lockouts, Newsom joined Unite Here union members on a picket line in front of the Westin St. Francis Hotel. He refused to allow sponsoring city events in them until the hotels agreed to a contract with workers; a contract was signed in September 2006. Newsom has taken leadership positions on gun safety, marijuana, the death penalty, universal health care, access to preschool, technology, criminal justice reform, and the minimum wage, in many cases leading to significant changes when his policies were ultimately accepted and replicated across the state and nation.
- **Dianne Feinstein** was serving as the (first female) president of San Francisco's Board of

Supervisors in 1978 when Mayor George Moscone and City Supervisor Harvey Milk were assassinated by Dan White. She succeeded Moscone as the (first woman) mayor of San Francisco and was seen as a moderate and a centrist. She was a major factor in bringing the 1984 Democratic National Convention to the city. She was elected to the Senate in 1992, along with Barbara Boxer; they were the first two women senators from California.

Feinstein's positions have continued to be centrist. She worked well with Governor Schwarzenegger and President George W. Bush, supported FISA and Patriot Act renewals, and talked about political compromises that could be made with the Trump administration. She introduced the Federal Assault Weapons Ban that was passed in 1994, and which expired in 2004; she was not successful in 2013, after the Sandy Hook Elementary School shooting, in her attempts to get the ban renewed. As a member of the Senate's Select Committee on Intelligence, she labeled the "enhanced interrogation" techniques used by the CIA as a "stain on our values and on our history." She was most recently re-elected, with 65% of the vote, in 2018, even though the state's Democratic committee saw her as not liberal enough.

- **Kamala Harris** serves as the junior US senator from California. She was elected to be the district attorney of San Francisco from 2004 to 2011, and the attorney general of California from 2011 until

2017. As a prosecutor, she specialized in child sexual abuse trials, difficult prosecutions, given that juries are more inclined to accept the word of an adult over the word of a child.

Harris supports single-payer healthcare, removing cannabis from the list of Schedule 1 drugs, a path to citizenship for undocumented immigrants, the DREAM Act, a ban on assault rifles, and lowering the tax burden for the working and middle classes while raising taxes on corporations and the wealthiest one percent of Americans. She is seen as more progressive than Feinstein and has gained recognition for her focused interrogations of nominees for such posts as the Supreme Court. She was a candidate for the Democratic nomination for the presidency in 2019 before withdrawing from the race.

- **Barbara Lee** has been serving as the Democratic US representative from Oakland and most of the northern part of Alameda County. She was co-chair of the Congressional Progressive Caucus (2005–2009), and is the vice chair and a founding member of the LGBT Equality Caucus. As detailed in chapter 5, she was the only member of Congress to vote against the authorization of use of force following the September 11 attacks, a position that the majority of the House has now moved to support.
- **Jackie Speier** has served in Congress since 2008, representing San Mateo County, which is just

south of San Francisco. Her literal initiation under fire came as she survived being shot five times when, as an aide to Congressman Leo Ryan, she was with him in 1978 when he was assassinated during his investigation of Jonestown. She has introduced legislation to end sexual assault in the military, at the service academies and in the halls of Congress. She was not successful in calling for an amendment to the National Defense Authorization Act for fiscal 2018 that would have required women to register for the draft.

- **London Breed**, the 45th mayor of San Francisco, was elected to the Board of Supervisors in 2012 and elected its president in 2015. Known as a hands-on manager, she has gathered real-time information by taking unannounced walks through different neighborhoods of the city and then taking action to address problems she saw. She made homelessness an early focus of her administration and has moved strongly to build an initial thousand shelter beds in new navigation centers.
- **Libby Schaaf** is serving her second term as mayor of Oakland. After serving on the Oakland City Council for four years, she won a highly contested election in 2014, and was reelected with 55% of the vote in 2018 over nine challengers. She is seen as successful in reducing violent crime in the city, and as being in touch with her large and diverse community. She also earned some measure of notoriety in 2018 when she was one of several city mayors who warned their constituents of

impending ICE immigration agent raids. The *New York Times* reported that her message for immigrants who are in Oakland illegally was this: "Your city wants you to be safe, wants to keep your family together and is proud to have you as part of our community." She also stepped forward to work with Governor Newsom to provide assistance to passengers trapped on a cruise ship at the onset of the coronavirus.

- **Jerry Brown** served as the 34th and 39th governor of California. During 1975 to 1983, he was (mostly affectionately) called "Governor Moonbeam," for his ahead-of-the-time liberal perspectives on such concepts as alternative energy and banning the death penalty, his fiscal conservatism, his interest in and study of Zen Buddhism, and his social involvement with entertainer Linda Ronstadt. In his second go-round as governor, between 2011 to 2019, he steered the state through and out of the major financial problems related to the recession that began in 2008. Between those terms as governor, he served as an effective mayor of Oakland from 1999 to 2007, and attorney general of California from 2007 to 2011.

- **Barbara Boxer** served as a member of the House of Representatives for ten years, and then as senator from 1993 to 2017. She was considered a liberal firebrand, and has been described as a forceful advocate for families, children, consumers, and the environment. At the same time, she worked across the aisle when possible, and she

and Oklahoma senator Jim Inhofe, who disagreed
on almost every issue, worked together to get a
water resources and infrastructure bill passed in
2007, with sufficient bipartisan support to over-
ride a presidential veto. In 2020, she joined a
Washington, DC, public affairs advising firm.

• **Willie Brown** is an attorney and former Speaker
of the California State Assembly. He completed 15
years as Speaker, where the *New York Times* had
called him one of the country's most powerful
state legislators. He was termed out after term
limits were introduced, after which he then ran for
and was elected to be the first African American
mayor of San Francisco. The *San Francisco
Chronicle* called Brown "one of San Francisco's
most notable mayors," adding that he had "celeb-
rity beyond the city's boundaries."

Brown served as San Francisco mayor from
January 8, 1996, until January 8, 2004. His tenure was marked by a significant increase in real
estate development, public works, city beauti-
fication, and other large-scale city projects. He
presided over the dot-com era at a time when
San Francisco's economy was rapidly expanding. Brown's administration included more Asian
Americans, women, Latinos, gays, and African
Americans than the administrations of his pre-
decessors. His credibility with all sectors of the
community, based on his transparent honesty, enabled him to solve a major port labor dispute because he was the only one all sides were willing to

trust. Brown has retired from formal politics, but his knowledge and wisdom continue to be sought by Democrats of all persuasions, and his Sunday column in the *San Francisco Chronicle* is considered by many to be their number one weekly read.

Getting America Back on Track

Should we only be tolerating each other's values, religious beliefs, traditions, and practices — or should we be embracing, sharing, and celebrating those differences? Can we find ways to diminish the active presence of hate that currently poisons our public discourse and our democracy?

While touring Rhode Island in 1790, after it became the 13th state to adopt the Constitution, George Washington stopped at the Touro Synagogue in Newport. Notables and officials of that city, and representatives from various religious groups, jockeyed for the honor of reading the president letters of welcome to their city.

Moses Seixas, an official of the Touro congregation, poured out his heart full of gratitude to George Washington for his leadership in the establishment of a new government, and he expressed his hope that this new country would accord all of its citizens respect and tolerance, whatever their background and religious beliefs.

The Seixas letter moved the president, and he responded with a letter of his own on August 21, 1790:

It is now no more that toleration is spoken of, as if it was by the indulgence of one class of people, that another enjoyed the exercise of their inherent natural rights.

For happily the Government of the United States gives to bigotry no sanction, to persecution no assistance, requires only that they who live under its protection should demean themselves as good citizens, in giving it on all occasions their effectual support. Everyone shall sit in safety under His own vine and fig tree, and there shall be none to make him afraid.

More than 225 years after Washington's letter, in 2017, Rex Tillerson was serving as the US secretary of state, the top US diplomat. He said:

It's simply important to say — although I think it's well understood and embraced, I'm certain, by everyone in this room — we all know hate is not an American value, nowhere is it an American value.

Arguments about "hate speech," speech designed to demean, challenge, or incite hatred of members of one group against another group, and against individuals within that "other" group, have been conflated with arguments about free speech. All sides claim to support free speech. Perhaps the question to be addressed is more one of why people are willing to tolerate by listening to, and sometimes adopting, hate-filled viewpoints.

The prayer of Saint Francis, who is the patron saint of San Francisco, addresses these concerns for all of us:

> Where there is hatred, let me sow love;
> Where there is injury, pardon;
> Where there is doubt, faith;
> Where there is despair, hope;
> Where there is darkness, light;
> And where there is sadness, joy.

James Carville and Mary Matalin are high-level political consultants who advise candidates on very different sides of the political aisle, yet who have also enjoyed a 20-plus year marriage together. In a conversation in which they discussed how they have been both personally and professionally successful with those sometimes vast differences in perspectives, they responded by saying that they each believed that the people who sought their advice and ran for seats of power were people who were dedicated to the welfare of the country and its people, that the differences were about how to achieve good ends for the country.

If one accepts that perspective, then perhaps individuals can focus more on separating, in their minds, those who are truly there to serve and improve our country from those who are there for less noble reasons.

To analyze and judge what is real, who is really doing what kinds of good and bad things, one needs to seek information, real and valid information. Perhaps to have and follow multiple news sources that don't all track back to the same political base, recognizing the wisdom of Congresswoman Eshoo's question at the head of this chapter. Perhaps to learn how to spot or at least question what might be dis-information from sources on any side. Perhaps also to suss out and reject the hypocrisy that is too often evident.

One example may be found when considering one of the issues not addressed in detail in this book: that of climate change. We know that not all of "science" is necessarily true. Many of us have been amused by scientific studies that tell us that a particular food is bad for us, only to be told later that it is in fact good for us, or vice versa. Most of us do know that the only absolute truth about food is that chocolate is always a good thing.

Galileo was considered a heretic by rulers, clerics, and scientists of his era for his support of Copernicus's scientific belief that the earth rotated around the sun; proof later evolved to support their accurate theses.

Nevertheless, when some politicians take a position, for example, on climate change that is based on politics rather than on the best available information, their sincerity can be questioned. When those politicians say, "Oh, I don't know, I'm not a scientist," but then they ignore or deny the information shared and the positions detailed by 98% of those who are scientists, the question of whether they are there for the people, or for themselves, or for their party, seems worth asking.

One can appreciate the irony when, in November 2019, the regional council chambers in Venice, Italy, were flooded for the first time in history, just after the council rejected measures to combat climate change.

Australia's prime minister, Scott Morrison, took office in 2018, with a commitment to polluting fossil fuels that was well known. In 2017, he brought a lump of coal to Parliament and presented it to his fellow members of that august body. "This is coal. Don't be afraid! Don't be scared! Won't hurt you," he said. He chose not to mention that the coal had been shellacked to prevent his hands from getting dirty.

In 2018, Morrison's country suffered major droughts, and the spring of 2019 was the driest on record. The Great Barrier Reef has already suffered extensive coral bleaching and death that has been attributed to climate change, and it is anticipated that the entire reef will die with just a couple of additional degrees of warming. In late 2019, a major portion of the Australian continent was ablaze, with widespread scientific consensus that the increase in temperatures that we have already seen — a global average of 1.1 degrees Celsius — has contributed to Australia's devastating fire season by creating ever-drier and hotter conditions. At the same time, Morrison was supporting a pro-fossil-fuel policy that included plans for a new coal-fired power plant, and the allocation of ten million dollars toward a study assessing whether to revive a decommissioned coal plant in Queensland.

Closer to home, the irony bell clanged when Florida governor Rick Scott's administration made it unacceptable to even have the phrase "climate change" on official websites or in governmental documentation, even as Miami continued to flood regularly.

When a 17-year-old Swedish schoolgirl understands the significance of climate science, and of the implications of that science for the need for massive global action, better than some people in high elected offices, one may have additional questions about the values and motivations of some of those in high office.

The United States was founded on the belief that all people are created equal. Equality is the bedrock of what America stands for, no matter where you live, who you love, and what your background in the country. San Francisco endorses those values along with the rest of the country.

Innovation has been a bedrock value in this new world. John Deere's brilliant mechanical work helped the American Midwest become a world leader in the production of food. We've looked at the contributions of San Francisco's computer and pharmaceutical technologies. Without innovation, we stand still or fall back. With innovation, we find new and better ways to live. We discover new medicines to heal our sick. These are values across the country, and shared research benefits us all.

Personal freedom, the rights to work, love, and live where and with whom we choose, and the rights to make medical decisions about our own bodies, and about the right to make our own decisions on who is allowed to touch our bodies medically or sexually (with affirmative consent) are also important in the country and world today.

Kentucky's law subjecting women to an unneeded medical procedure and emotional harassment before they can obtain an abortion, and a number of similar laws recently passed in other states, do not respect that personal freedom. A bill introduced into Ohio's state legislature in 2019 requiring the "reimplantation" of the embryo in an ectopic pregnancy goes against medical knowledge — doctors call it medically impossible. This is an attempted imposition of a procedure that is both emotionally cruel and physically dangerous upon individuals by the state.

Americans tend to support our military personnel, even as questions about military actions and military adventures can and should very legitimately be questioned. Blind obedience to authority is neither an American nor a San Francisco value. Loyalty to our nation and our form of government is something we do value, and we need to maintain the strength to stand clearly on issues that could harm us or diminish our society. We need to be open to learn from our mistakes, such as in military actions like Vietnam and Iraq, and to question and consider before acting. Support for our allies also tends to gain approval of most of us.

We have been a nation with a very mixed record on our treatment of various national and racial groups. Yet we are a nation of ethnically and racially mixed people, and the history of the United States is in all our genes. We do need to create fair and comprehensive immigration policies and methodologies as we move forward, with "E pluribus unum" as a guiding principle, to maintain our own humanity and the strength of this country.

So, yes, these are American values, and these are San Francisco values, the values that are entrenched in our democracy. The values that we all need to part of re-establishing, by drawing upon the Take Action steps detailed in at the end of each chapter. Robert Kennedy's words can perhaps guide each of us as we work to get our country back on track:

> Moral courage is a rarer commodity than bravery in battle or great intelligence. Yet it is the one essential vital quality for those who seek to change a world that yields most painfully to change.

We need to continue to be able to express our opinions freely to each other and to our government, with dialog that is not hate-based. We need to support the understanding that, as long as we are not imposing our beliefs upon another person, all Americans can express and live our freedoms. That may be the ultimate San Francisco value.

The Authors

About Geri Spieler

Investigative journalist and native Californian Geri Spieler has lived in the San Francisco Bay Area for the past 25 years. She has chaired the Jack London Writers Conference and served as president of the California Writers Club San Francisco/Peninsula Branch; she has now returned to the board, serving as vice president for programs. She is a member of the Women's National Book Association, the Society of Professional Journalists, the Association of Internet Research Specialists, the National Book Critics Circle, and the Internet Society.

Prior to writing *San Francisco Values*, Spieler published *Taking Aim at the President: The Remarkable Story of the Woman Who Shot at Gerald Ford* (Palgrave Macmillan), which has won four literary awards, including first places at both the San Francisco and Hollywood Book Festivals, second place at the San Francisco Writers Conference, and the Mensa Sharp Book Lovers First Place Award for non-fiction. *Taking Aim at the President* has been optioned for a movie by screen writers and executive producers Taylor Allen and Andrew Logan.

Spieler is also a freelance writer for print and on-line publications. She has written for the *San Francisco Chronicle*, *Los Angeles Times*, *Huffington Post*, *Forbes*, and

Truthdig. She published more than 150 research articles on technology as a Gartner analyst and has been a regular reviewer for the *New York Journal of Books.*

In addition to a robust writing career, Spieler maintains a fruit orchard for canning and shares the abundant fruit with local food banks. She also raises chickens exclusively for their eggs; each chicken has name, and they are her pets. Spieler also serves a first responder with the local Santa Clara County Community Emergency Response Team. Geri was named "Big Sister of the Year" during her time in Washington, DC. She and her husband and co-author, Rick Kaplowitz, live in Palo Alto, California.

About Rick Kaplowitz, EdD

Dr. Kaplowitz has served as a senior executive in academia and in technology. He was a dean and vice president at colleges including Rutgers University, Merrimack College, New England Institute, and the Pacific Graduate School of Psychology. He was a director at Raytheon (Defense Systems division) and a vice president at Gartner (technology consulting).

Rick has been involved in the management of local political campaigns in both Andover, Massachusetts, and Palo Alto, California. He has also served on community boards, including on the Santa Clara County Senior Care Commission; California Senior Leadership Alliance; Billy DeFrank Center; Leadership Palo Alto; Adolescent Counseling Services; and Greater Lawrence Mental Health & Retardation Board.

A Silicon Valley resident for the past 30 years, Rick grew up on a dead-end street in Brooklyn. He earned his bachelor's degree at Brooklyn College and his master's degree at Columbia University, taught mathematics in Brooklyn and in France, and then attended Harvard University, where he earned his doctorate, studying at the schools of education and management.

Rick's publications have focused primarily on personnel processes in academia, including: "Selecting Academic Administrators: The Search Committee" (American Council on Education), "Recruitment, Appointment, Promotion and Termination of Academic Personnel" (in the *International Encyclopedia of Higher Education*, Jossey-Bass), and "Selecting College and University Personnel: The Quest and the Questions" (Association for the Study of Higher Education).

An accomplished public speaker, Rick finds that his speaking these days is well received at marriage celebrations, where he serves as a wedding officiant. He and his wife and co-author, Geri Spieler, live in Palo Alto, California.

CPSIA information can be obtained
at www.ICGtesting.com
Printed in the USA
LVHW030602220720
661196LV00005B/387